SEED THOUGHTS
Devotional

SEED THOUGHTS
Devotional

ENCOURAGEMENT FOR OUR LIVES

by
Lynette Hagin

Unless otherwise indicated, all Scripture quotations are taken from the *King James Version* of the Bible.

Scripture quotations marked AMP are taken from *The Amplified Bible*, Old Testament copyright © 1965, 1987 by the Zondervan Corporation. The Amplified New Testament copyright © 1958, 1987 by The Lockman Foundation. Used by permission.

Scripture quotations marked MSG are taken from *The Message*. Copyright © 1993, 1994, 1995, 1996, 2000, 2001, 2002. Used by permission of NavPress Publishing Group.

Scripture quotations marked NIV are taken from the *Holy Bible, New International Version*®. NIV®. Copyright © 1973, 1978, 1984 by International Bible Society. Used by permission of Zondervan. All rights reserved.

Scripture quotations marked NKJV are taken from the *New King James Version*. Copyright © 1982 by Thomas Nelson, Inc. Used by permission. All rights reserved.

Scripture quotations marked NLT are taken from the *Holy Bible, New Living Translation*, copyright © 1996, 2004. Used by permission of Tyndale House Publishers, Inc., Wheaton, IL 60189 USA. All rights reserved.

Scripture quotations marked TLB are taken from *The Living Bible* copyright © 1971. Used by permission of Tyndale House Publishers, Inc., Wheaton, IL 60189. All rights reserved.

15 14 13 12 11 10 09 08   08 07 06 05 04 03 02 01

Seed Thoughts Devotional: Encouragement for Our Lives
ISBN-13: 978-0-89276-804-2
ISBN-10: 0-89276-804-5

In the U.S. write:
Kenneth Hagin Ministries
P.O. Box 50126
Tulsa, OK 74150-0126
1-888-28-FAITH
www.rhema.org

In Canada write:
Kenneth Hagin Ministries
P.O. Box 335, Station D
Etobicoke (Toronto), Ontario
Canada, M9A 4X3
1-866-70-RHEMA
www.rhemacanada.org

CONTENTS

INTRODUCTION

God has planned a wonderful and beautiful life for us all. However, the most important thing that we must do is commit our life to Him and allow Him to direct our steps. The following scripture has ministered to me on a daily basis: *"The steps of a good man are ordered by the Lord: and he delighteth in his way. Though he fall, he shall not be utterly cast down: for the Lord upholdeth him with his hand"* (Ps. 37:23–24).

When I started my journey in life with God, committed to walk in His ways, it was beyond my comprehension exactly what He had planned for me. If He had given me the plan ahead of time, I would have quit before I ever began. However, I am so thankful that He leads us one step at a time.

I am sure that you have been in the place where I have often found myself—wondering how I was going to accomplish the task or overcome the challenge that was before me. During such times, God has ministered just the right words in the right season to get me over the hurdle that was before me.

Sometimes He would give me a simple phrase such as, "You can make it." Other times I might read a plaque inscribed with just the thought I needed for the moment. I remember one particularly grave time in my life when I was tempted to panic about the situation at hand. I looked around the office in which I was standing and suddenly saw a plaque with the following words: "The task ahead of you is not greater than the force behind you." I sighed with relief, knowing that God was in control of the situation and His power was greater than any problem that I might find myself facing.

In this book I have compiled what I call "Seed Thoughts"—brief words of inspiration to help you overcome the daily challenges and stresses of life. These words are not merely something that I have thought up; they were given to me by the Lord in my moments of reaching out to Him for encouragement and strength.

This devotional contains 52 Seed Thoughts, one for each week of the year. I encourage you to take a thought and read it every day for one week. Educators have found that it takes reviewing something continually for it to become an automatic and routine part of our lives. You will find that as you read a Seed Thought for an entire week, God will speak to your heart on a daily basis. Similarly, as I have read the same scripture over and over, I have found something in that passage that I did not see in previous readings.

So I encourage you to find a moment each day when you can get alone with God. I like to sit in my favorite chair, light a candle, and take a few minutes to hear His daily instructions. I trust that these Seed Thoughts will minister encouragement to you. My favorite scripture is Philippians 4:13, *"I can do all things through Christ which strengtheneth me."* Throughout my life, He has strengthened me time and time again to do what may have seemed impossible. As you and God work together, watch impossibilities become possibilities in your life, as well.

◌

New Year, New Life

"Brethren, I count not myself to have apprehended: but this one thing I do, forgetting those things which are behind, and reaching forth unto those things which are before."

Philippians 3:13

Embarking upon a new year means having the opportunity to start out the year with a clean slate. Before us lies a new beginning. Regardless of what last year brought—whether it was a good year or a challenging year for us—it is now history, and history cannot be changed. So it does not profit us to live in memories of the past.

We cannot move forward by looking back, which is why so many Christians live below their privileges. They constantly allow the devil to remind them of past mistakes.

The Apostle Paul knew from experience the importance of *"forgetting those things which are behind."* He had a lot to forget.

I'm sure the enemy tried quite frequently to remind him of how he had persecuted the Christians before his conversion. Those thoughts could have tormented him, but Paul chose to leave the past behind and *"press toward the mark for the prize of the high calling of God in Christ Jesus"* (v. 14).

If you have asked the Heavenly Father to forgive you of your wrongdoings, those blemishes have now been removed from your account and you can *"press toward the mark"* too. According to 1 John 1:7 and 9, the blood of Jesus has cleansed you from all unrighteousness. So don't allow the enemy to keep you in condemnation regarding your past. When thoughts of condemnation come knocking at your door, remember what Paul said in Philippians 3:13–14 and press forward.

Something else Paul chose to do was to *forget* the way others had persecuted him because of his stand for Christ, and to *forgive* them. Paul told us in Ephesians 4:31–32, *"Let all bitterness, and wrath, and anger, and clamour, and evil speaking, be put away from you, with all malice: And be ye kind one to another, tenderhearted, forgiving one another, even as God for Christ's sake hath forgiven you."* Why is it so important to not only forgive ourselves, but to forgive others for offenses committed against us?

Some people will never progress in life or fulfill God's plan for them because they choose to dwell on past mistakes or on the offenses of others.

I don't want you to be one of them. I encourage you this day to let go of the past. Let go of any bitter feelings toward those who have offended you. Let go of any hurts you may be experiencing because of past abuse in your life. Forgive the parents who may have abandoned you as a child. The Lord cannot forgive them for you. *You* must willingly choose to forgive and forget and to let go of grudges and bitterness. The only way for you to experience healing from your past is to choose to forgive and forget.

When you begin a new year—a new day, a new month, a new season of life—with a clean slate, as one who has forgiven and forgotten, you can experience a peace and joy that you have not known before. You can expect the wall of hurt and disappointment that may have been built around you to begin to crumble. And you can look for contentment, unlike anything you've experienced before, to encompass you. Life will have new meaning as you begin to enjoy the abundant blessings that God has for you!

Prayer:

Heavenly Father, in Jesus' Name, I am choosing today to forgive everyone in my past who has done or said anything to hurt me, including myself. I want to progress in life. With Your help I am going to press forward and live the abundant life that You have planned for me.

Thoughts for the Week:

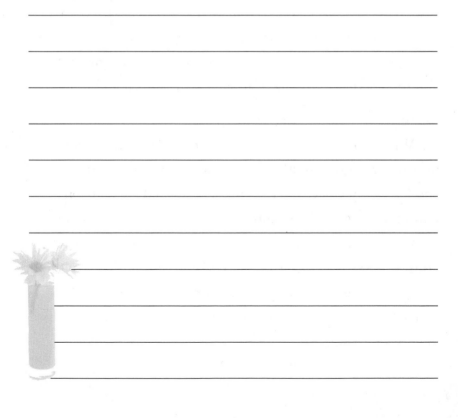

_____

_____

_____

_____

_____

_____

_____

_____

_____

_____

⌒

Good Success

"Then thou shalt make thy way prosperous, and then thou shalt have good success."

Joshua 1:8

It seems impossible that another year has come and gone. You may be thinking, *With the help of the Lord, I made it through the year!* But remember that last year is history and you now can look to this new year with anticipation. So what kind of New Year's resolutions have you made?

One thing that each of us desires is to have a successful and prosperous life. God has given us His formula for success in the Book of Joshua, and it relates to what I believe the Lord is calling us all to in this next year—a greater commitment from us to spend quality time in the Word of God and to put His Word into practice.

After the death of Moses, the Lord told the Israelites:

JOSHUA 1:8
This book of the law shall not depart out of thy mouth; but thou shalt meditate therein day and night, that thou mayest observe to do according to all that is written therein: for then thou shalt make thy way prosperous, and then thou shalt have good success.

Notice that the Lord is not just talking about success here, but *good* success! This verse tells us that to have good success we need to meditate in the Word continually and practice the Word of God in our lives.

Many Christians include the same items in their New Year's resolutions every year: to study the Word more diligently and practice it in their daily lives, and to spend more time in prayer. Yet, if we're not careful, the enemy (Satan) will subtly begin to steal our time, and before we know it, we will find ourselves too busy in the natural to spend time with the Lord. This year, I want to encourage you not to let Satan rob you of the one thing that will make you a success in life.

While "good success" can refer to those who obey God not lacking anything that is good, keep in mind that success is more than just personal gain.

As the Body of Christ, we have a great work to do. Matthew 9:37–38 says, *"The harvest truly is plenteous, but the labourers are few; Pray ye therefore the Lord of the harvest, that he will send forth labourers into his harvest."* I believe we are living in the last days, and the Lord needs laborers to bring in the end-time harvest. Each of us can be a laborer in the harvest field. What greater success than to bring others into the Kingdom!

I encourage you to make being a witness in your world one of your New Year's resolutions. Whatever your world encompasses— your neighbors, coworkers, family, or people you meet on the street—pray for opportunities to share the Gospel with them.

One way we all have to witness to others about God is just by living a godly life. I'm sure you have heard the old adage, "Actions speak louder than words." It's important that we be good witnesses through our actions. Often that is a choice we must make. For instance, say someone cuts in front of me in a store line. My flesh may want to react a certain way, but I simply smile and say, "You must be in a hurry. Please go ahead of me" (even when I'm in a hurry too). A simple gesture like that can open the door for witnessing.

Psalm 37:23 says, *"The steps of a good man are ordered by the Lord: and he delighteth in his way."* Let the Lord guide your steps this year. Be sensitive to His promptings. Many times we miss a good opportunity because we are not sensitive to the voice of God (which we can hear in our heart and through His Word).

God's Word says that He can do exceeding abundantly above all that you could ask or think, according to the power that is at work in you (Eph. 3:20). I believe this new year holds great abundance for you if you will dare to trust and believe God and study and practice His Word. As you allow the Lord to lead and guide you throughout the year, I know that you will have "good success" as He brings His Word to pass in your life!

Prayer:

Father God, this new year I want to be a laborer in the end-time harvest field. Help me to be sensitive to Your guidance and take advantage of every opportunity to be a witness and share the Gospel with everyone in my world, in the Name of Jesus.

Thoughts for the Week:

WEEK 3

Who's at the Helm?

"Trust in the Lord with all your heart and lean not on your own understanding; in all your ways acknowledge him, and he will make your paths straight."

Proverbs 3:5–6 NIV

I love the song by Andrae Crouch[1] that talks about what we can learn through all our trials and troubles: to trust in Jesus and to depend on the Word.[2] How true those words should ring in our hearts! Our friends may fail us, and our family may fail us—but Jesus never fails! He will see us through the fiercest storm in life. When we get into the boat with Him, we can trust His words, *"Let us go over to the other side"* (Mark 4:35 NIV).

I believe that the Lord is bringing each of us to a place of absolute trust in Him. It is essential that we place a greater trust in Him than ever before. We must not allow trusting God to become our last resort.

9

King David knew how to trust his God. He wrote in Psalm 18:2–3, *"The Lord is my rock, and my fortress, and my deliverer; my God, my strength, in whom I will trust; my buckler, and the horn of my salvation, and my high tower. I will call upon the Lord, who is worthy to be praised: so shall I be saved from mine enemies."*

David knew how to commit his entire life to the Lord. Sometimes we attempt to handle our situations all by ourselves. Yet the Lord is willing and able to help us through any circumstance that may come our way. It is so important that we commit our entire life to Him. Proverbs 3:5–6 says, *"Trust in the Lord with all your heart and lean not on your own understanding; in all your ways acknowledge him, and he will make your paths straight"* (NIV).

I admonish you to place your entire trust in God this year if you haven't already done so. Let Him direct your paths. Sometimes that is difficult for us, because we would like to see the whole picture. But God does not operate that way. He usually shows us His plans one step at a time. Walking with Him is a daily step of faith. Second Corinthians 5:7 says, *"We live by faith, not by sight"* (NIV).

When you try to figure things out with your own understanding, your mind will give you fits! That is why it is so important to keep your mind on the Lord. Let Him direct your paths. We often try to figure out how God is going to work everything out. It is important that we just stand back, lean on Him, and trust Him to work out every situation for our good. I encourage you to read Romans 8:28 and insert your name into the scripture. This is how I read it for myself: "And we know that all things work together for Lynette's good because she loves God and is called according to His purpose."

Start putting your name in the Scriptures. They will take on a new meaning for you. As you commit your life to the Lord and walk in His plan, you can be assured that He will work out all things for your good, just as He promises in His Word.

When you begin to understand trusting in God, you'll begin to experience the peace of God in your life. The Scriptures admonish us in Colossians 3:15, *"Let the peace of Christ rule in your hearts, since as members of one body you were called to peace. And be thankful"* (NIV). When you allow the Lord to be at the helm of your ship, you can walk in peace. Though your boat may be going through some rough waters, you can rest in peace, knowing that the Lord Jesus Christ will get you to the other side!

Determine this year to wholly follow God and live a consecrated, dedicated, and holy life before Him. Place your trust in Him—knowing that whatever circumstances may come your way, He will see you through—and you will experience His matchless peace in your life!

Prayer:

Father God, I'm ready to stop trying to figure things out all the time with my own understanding. I commit my life to You. Help me to keep my mind on You and trust You to work out every situation for my good, in the Name of Jesus.

Thoughts for the Week:

Change Worries
Into Prayer

"Don't fret or worry. Instead of worrying, pray. Let petitions and praises shape your worries into prayers, letting God know your concerns. Before you know it, a sense of God's wholeness, everything coming together for good, will come and settle you down."

Philippians 4:6–7 MSG

Stress is running rampant in our world and it's an important issue that Christians face as well. One survey I heard of reported that 89 percent of the respondents described experiencing "high levels of stress" regularly. Medical experts say that stress is the cause of 80 percent of all human illness and disease. At the very least, it has a detrimental effect on our health. Those are alarming statistics.

Stress is actually closely related to worry. The Bible has much to say about worry as in Philippians 4:6: *"Do not fret or*

*have any anxiety about anything, but in every circumstance and in
everything, by prayer and petition (definite requests), with thanksgiving, continue to make your wants known to God"* (AMP). To deal
with stress, you must identify the cause. Here are two common
causes that I dealt with personally.

When I was in my 40s, I suddenly found that I was tired all
the time. That was not normal for me. I had always been full of
energy. At first I thought perhaps the problem was my age. I had
heard people say that as you get older, you have to slow down.
Then quite by accident, I found the real reason.

One day, my husband and I decided to get away for a few
days for some much needed rest. We enjoyed riding four-wheel-
ers, so we went to the sand dunes in western Oklahoma and
rode our bikes. Nothing can be more exhausting than that kind
of workout, yet I found I had an abundance of energy for recre-
ation, which puzzled me. So in my prayer time, I began to ask
the Lord for the answer to my dilemma.

Suddenly my answer came. I had assumed the management
of several areas at our ministry and my new duties included
major decision making. I realized I was uncomfortable making
decisions for this new responsibility. I felt stressed from it, and
the physical result was a drastic decrease of my energy.

I immediately said to the Lord, "I'm going to eliminate this stress by claiming James 1:5 when I must make decisions." I like the *New Living Translation* of this verse, which reads, *"If you need wisdom, ask our generous God, and he will give it to you. He will not rebuke you for asking."* That was 20 years ago. I have not stressed over decisions since then, nor has my energy decreased.

Another cause of stress is *facing unexpected interruptions in your schedule*. Being a perfectionist, I would become stressed when things did not go according to plan. Once again, I came to realize it was senseless to worry about something when you can do nothing about it. I learned that when a friend and I drove to Branson, Missouri, to take care of some ministry business.

We had planned to be gone just one night, so I took very little luggage. I did not take my computer or any of my paperwork. We were on our way back to Tulsa when icy road conditions forced us to stop in Joplin, Missouri. We were stuck there for three days! I did not even have an ice scraper in my car, and I had worn shoes that were not appropriate for that icy weather.

I could have easily stressed out about that situation. Instead, I laughed and said, "Lord, I guess You have a real sense of humor. I suppose this is the only way You could get me to slow down and just pamper myself." And that's just what I did! I spent those three days catching up on my sleep and relaxing. When we finally returned to Tulsa, I felt totally rested and refreshed.

I want to encourage you to rest in the Lord. Let Him work out the situations in your life. He will give you wisdom and strength to perform the tasks you encounter on a daily basis.

Prayer:

Father, forgive me for worrying and being anxious about anything. I don't want to be stressed anymore. Please give me the wisdom and strength for each task I need to perform. Help me to rest in You every day and let You work out the situations in my life, in the Name of Jesus.

Thoughts for the Week:

Choose to Live Victoriously

"I have set before you life and death, blessing and cursing; therefore choose life, that . . . you . . . may live."

Deuteronomy 30:19 NKJV

Recently I came across a story that really spoke to me. A little boy was overheard talking to himself as he strutted through the backyard wearing his baseball cap and toting a ball and bat. "I'm the greatest hitter in the world," he announced. Then he tossed the ball into the air, swung at it, and missed. "Strike one!" he yelled.

Undaunted, he picked up the ball and said again, "I'm the greatest hitter in the world!" He tossed the ball into the air. When it came down, he swung again and missed. "Strike two!" he cried. The boy then paused a moment to examine his bat and ball carefully. He spit on his hands and rubbed them together.

He straightened his cap and said once more, "I'm the greatest hitter in the world!" Again he tossed the ball up in the air and swung at it. He missed. "Strike three! Wow!" the boy exclaimed, "I'm the greatest pitcher in the world!"

I love that story because it shows how our attitude determines how circumstances impact our life. This little boy's circumstances hadn't changed, but his optimistic attitude prompted him to give encouraging meaning to what had happened. Perhaps last year brought some negative situations into your life. Perhaps it caused you to have attitude issues. If so, I encourage you to begin this new year by getting a complete overhaul in your attitudes.

It is challenging to constantly keep our attitude in check, but if we aren't careful, we can have what some call "stinking thinking." It is true that life is not always fair. We can choose to cry over our circumstances, or we can choose to live victoriously in spite of them. When it comes to attitudes, two Bible characters to whom I often refer are King David and the Apostle Paul.

When you look at their lives, you will find that both men found themselves in many difficult circumstances. In those situations, David continually cried out to his God. When he was surrounded by enemies, he wrote in Psalm 56:3–4, *"What time I am afraid, I will trust in thee. In God I will praise his word, in God I have put my trust; I will not fear what flesh can do unto me."* And in verse 9 he said, *"When I cry unto thee, then shall mine enemies turn back: this I know; for God is for me."* If David had taken the attitude, "My enemies are going to destroy me," he would have been destroyed. He didn't get into "stinking thinking." Instead, he kept his focus on his deliverer, the Lord God.

The Apostle Paul also encountered many difficult situations in his life. He was beaten, stoned, shipwrecked, and imprisoned for the sake of the Gospel. Yet he expressed a positive attitude in Second Corinthians 2:14, saying, *"Now thanks be unto God, which always causeth us to triumph in Christ, and maketh manifest the savour of his knowledge by us in every place."* Regardless of the circumstances that Paul found himself in, he kept the attitude that, in Christ, he could triumph.

In life we need to maintain the attitudes that both King David and the Apostle Paul possessed. We may not be surrounded by enemies, and we may not have been literally beaten, but perhaps the circumstances in our lives have beaten us down.

I want to encourage you today—keep your eyes on your Heavenly Father. In Him you will find strength, peace, and help to bring you out of every circumstance in your life. That is what Jesus was saying in John 16:33 (AMP): *"I have told you these things, so that in Me you may have [perfect] peace and confidence. In the world you have tribulation and trials and distress and frustration; but be of good cheer [take courage; be confident, certain, undaunted]! For I have overcome the world. [I have deprived it of power to harm you and have conquered it for you.]"*

Regardless of the situations that you may encounter this year, choose to adjust your attitude. Realize that you can relax and enjoy life because the Lord is on your side, and He is working on your behalf to turn every situation around for your good.

Prayer:

Lord, help me turn my thoughts to the positive things in life rather than the negative. And help me always keep the attitude that in You I can triumph, in the Name of Jesus.

Thoughts for the Week:

_____

_____

_____

_____

The Importance
of Ministering

"Each of you should look not only to your own interests, but also to the interests of others."

Philippians 2:4 NIV

Living in such a busy world, we often forget the importance of ministering to one another. We get so wrapped up in our own concerns that we become insensitive to those around us who are hurting. Yet we are told in the Bible to look out for them too. Are we so busy that we don't have time to minister to others?

We have all been guilty at times of allowing our agendas to take first place in our lives. When I am tempted to place my priorities above God's priorities, a scripture instilled in me by my parents rings in my ear: *"But seek ye first the kingdom of God, and his righteousness; and all these things shall be added unto you"* (Matt. 6:33). When I don't have enough time to accomplish all that needs to be done, I say, "Lord, I'm going to place Your things first, and I expect You to show me how to redeem my time."

Let me relate a personal experience that proves God will take care of us if we will take care of His assignments.

A friend and I had made plans to go to Dallas, Texas, on a business trip. We had budgeted every minute, knowing that good time management was necessary for us to accomplish all that needed to be done. The day we were to go, a member of RHEMA Bible Church was involved in a terrible motorcycle accident in the Fort Worth, Texas, area. She was admitted to the hospital in very serious condition. My husband said to me as we were leaving, "Please try to go by the hospital and pray for our church member."

Of course, I desired to do that, but at first I thought, *Lord, how am I going to get everything done that must be done and go to the hospital as well? Besides, Lord, I am going to Dallas, not Fort Worth.* Then I thought about my priorities, remembering that my first assignment from God is to care for people. So I said, "Lord, please show me how to manage my time so that I can accomplish everything." I left the matter in His hands and began to schedule my day with His help.

We planned to drive to Fort Worth from Dallas that afternoon. In the natural, that didn't make sense since the traffic is normally heavy during that time. But it seemed to be the schedule the Lord was directing us to follow. So after accomplishing what we needed to in Dallas, we set out for Fort Worth with a map and a prayer, knowing that God would have to direct our path because neither of us could interpret maps accurately!

As we drove toward Fort Worth, we were amazed at how light the traffic was at five in the afternoon. We soon arrived without incident, but suddenly our map instructions ended and we were not at our destination. Knowing that time was short, I happened to notice that our rental car was equipped with a global positioning system (a GPS device) that was labeled "Never Lost."

Neither of us is good with computers, and we had no idea how to operate the system. So once again I prayed and said, "Lord, this machine says it is never lost, so help me to operate it." I began to push buttons, trying to find the right combination to obtain the information we needed. Suddenly, the right information appeared, and we were on our way to the hospital.

Once we arrived, we wondered how we were going to find our church member's room in such a large hospital. Again, we prayed and asked the Lord to direct us to the correct wing of the hospital. Then we walked into a lobby, and her husband was standing right there! My mouth dropped open because I didn't think he knew we were coming. So I asked him about it and he said, "No, but something on the inside said, 'Go to the lobby.'" Thank God for the Holy Ghost, Who will lead and direct us if we will but ask!

Needless to say, the lady rejoiced that we came to visit and pray for her. And I was ecstatic that the Lord had done exactly as we had asked, directing our steps and enabling us to accomplish all that we had set out to do. It once again confirmed to me that if we will put God's priorities first, He will take care of us and our every need!

Prayer:

Father God, forgive me for getting so wrapped up in my concerns that I am not sensitive to the needs of others. Help me to allow ministering to hurting people around me to take first place in my life. And when I do, thank You for showing me how to redeem my time, in the Name of Jesus.

Thoughts for the Week:

_____

_____

_____

_____

WEEK 7

∕⟋

'I Love You'

"Love . . . is patient and kind. . . . Love (God's love in us) . . .
is ever ready to believe the best of every person. . . . "

1 Corinthians 13:4–5, 7 AMP

Whenever I think of February, I think of love and Valentine's
Day. February 14 is a day when many people celebrate the love
of their life, and it is certainly wonderful to do that. Yet it is
more important that we learn to practice love in our life on a
daily basis. That doesn't seem to happen much in this genera-
tion, but it is scriptural.

Many people refer to First Corinthians 13 as "the love
chapter." Too often, we want to skip over reading that part of
the Bible. I admit I have felt that way at times, but the Lord still
continued to lead me to read it. In fact, whenever my husband
and I perform a marriage ceremony, I always read this portion of
chapter 13 to the bride and groom:

1 CORINTHIANS 13:4–7 AMP

4 Love endures long and is patient and kind; love never is envious nor boils over with jealousy, is not boastful or vainglorious, does not display itself haughtily.

5 It is not conceited (arrogant and inflated with pride); it is not rude (unmannerly) and does not act unbecomingly. Love (God's love in us) does not insist on its own rights or its own way, for it is not self-seeking; it is not touchy or fretful or resentful; it takes no account of the evil done to it [it pays no attention to a suffered wrong].

6 It does not rejoice at injustice and unrighteousness, but rejoices when right and truth prevail.

7 Love bears up under anything and everything that comes, is ever ready to believe the best of every person, its hopes are fadeless under all circumstances, and it endures everything [without weakening].

If we would practice this passage daily, we could live peaceful, productive lives. The problem is, our flesh often gets in the way. Instead of ignoring injustices that are done to us, we want to get even; instead of walking in love, we want to repay evil for evil.

One of the things I witnessed in the life of my father-in-law, Kenneth E. Hagin, was that he not only taught about the love walk, he truly lived it. He never considered getting even. At times, my husband and I got exasperated when we heard others criticize and say hurtful things about our family or ministry. Sometimes we expressed our feelings to my father-in-law, but he would tell us, "Don't ever stoop to their level; always walk the high road." I'm forever grateful for his example and for being straightforward with us. I still hear those words ringing in my ears when I'm tempted to walk the low road and return evil for evil.

The test of walking in love is not something you pass one time and never have to experience again. The fact is, your love walk will be tested continually. Sometimes it seems as if I experience those kinds of tests on a daily basis! There's a story I have heard about a woman who was complaining to her husband that he never told her he loved her. His answer was, "I told you I loved you when I asked you to marry me, and if I ever change my mind, I'll let you know." Of course, we should not be like that husband. We should say "I love you" freely. I believe those are vitally important words to say.

My husband and I make it a point to say "I love you" to each other many times a day, and I often say that to my children and grandchildren. We all need to be reassured of the love others have for us, and we need to reassure others of our love for them.

You may not have heard anyone say to you "I love you" very often in your childhood, and you may find it awkward to say those words yourself. But I want to encourage you that if you'll start saying "I love you" to people you care about, each time you repeat those words, they will become easier to say and more natural to you.

I encourage you not to take your friends and family for granted, but to express your love and appreciation for them on a continual basis. Don't live with regret after the death of a loved one, wishing you had expressed words of love to them more often. Begin right now with the determination that every day—not just on Valentine's Day—you will walk in love and express words of love to your family and friends.

Prayer:

When I think of Your love for me, Lord, I am overwhelmed! I'm going to start seeking to walk in love on a daily basis and express my love verbally for my loved ones, beginning with You—Jesus, I love You!

Thoughts for the Week:

_____

_____

_____

_____

Misplaced Confidence

"Fear nothing. . . . Because God's your refuge, the High God your very own home, Evil can't get close to you, harm can't get through the door."

Psalm 91:5, 9–10 MSG

With all that's going on in the world, it is very easy to become gripped with fear. Fear is a spirit that will try to control us to the point where we are afraid to function in our everyday lives. And fear will dominate us if we let it. Each of us has areas in our life where we have to deal with fear. When I am tempted to be afraid, I find a scripture to hold on to that will dissipate that fear.

Psalm 91 is one of the chapters in the Bible that I stand on for many areas of my life. I especially like the way *The Amplified Bible* translates it. For instance, Psalm 91:1 says, *"He who dwells in the secret place of the Most High shall remain stable and fixed under the shadow of the Almighty [Whose power no foe can withstand]."*

It is important that we place God first in our lives if we want to claim the promise of this scripture. Too many times, we expect God to hold up His end of the bargain when we are not doing our part. God's promises always have attached conditions. If you follow His conditions, then He is obligated to perform His Word.

I used to be frightened when my husband traveled and I was alone at night. Fear would torment me so fiercely that I would literally lay the Bible by my bed, opened to Psalm 91:5, which says, *"You shall not be afraid of the terror of the night, nor of the arrow (the evil plots and slanders of the wicked) that flies by day"* (AMP). When I awoke with fear, I read Psalm 91 and went back to sleep, trusting the Lord for His promise.

Whenever you are dealing with some kind of fear, I strongly encourage you to stand upon Psalm 91:5 and boldly proclaim that you will not be afraid of the evil plots and slanders of the wicked. Place your confidence in the Word of the Lord, which continues in Psalm 91:9–11, saying, *"Because you have made the Lord your refuge, and the Most High your dwelling place, There shall no evil befall you, nor any plague or calamity come near your tent. For He will give His angels [especial] charge over you to accompany and defend and preserve you in all your ways [of obedience and service]"* (AMP).

Whenever fear tries to come on you, boldly proclaim, "No evil can befall me, for my guardian angel is keeping me in all my ways. He is right beside me to protect me and keep harm from coming near me."

If your children are afraid, do as Jesus did when He spoke in parables and speak to them in a way they can understand. Children need to know that God is their Protector. We need to tell them in a way they can relate to and comprehend. I remember when our daughter, Denise, was around 10, she started waking up at night, crying and saying she was afraid. Each night, my husband would pray for her and tell her that she didn't have to be afraid because the Lord was protecting her. This went on for many weeks until one night after praying with her, he seemed impressed to tell her about her guardian angel.

Denise always slept with the stuffed animals her dad brought back to her from his travels. One of her favorites was a large tiger that she kept at the foot of her bed. That particular night as her dad was comforting her and endeavoring to get her to return to sleep, he said, "Denise, you have a guardian angel who sits beside you on your stuffed tiger while you sleep. So whenever you awaken and are frightened, just remember that your angel is here and you do not have to be afraid anymore." Denise was able to relate to that, and from that night on, she was not afraid.

You don't have to live in fear; you can live in peace. Isaiah 26:3 says, *"Thou wilt keep him in perfect peace, whose mind is stayed on thee: because he trusteth in thee."* I encourage you to keep your mind fixed on Jesus, for He is the Prince of Peace.

Prayer:

Lord, forgive me for succumbing to fear instead of focusing on You and exercising my faith in Your ability to protect me from all harm. Thank You that I am able to cast all my cares and fears upon You and walk through life in the abundance of Your peace, in the Name of Jesus.

Thoughts for the Week:

_____

_____

_____

_____

_____

_____

Steps of Success

"In all thy ways acknowledge him, and he shall direct thy paths."

Proverbs 3:6

I remember how excited Ken and I were as parents when our children took their first steps. They took one step and then fell down. So we picked them up, put them back on their feet, and encouraged them to take another step. Inspired by our words of encouragement, our children tried again. The next time, they took two or three steps before falling. But we repeated the process of picking them up, encouraging them, and helping them try again until they had finally conquered the task of walking.

Infants would never learn to walk if they didn't start by taking that first step. Just as an infant learns to walk one step at a time, so it is with God's plan for our lives. He doesn't show us the whole picture all at once because we may quit before we ever get started. If I had known 40 years ago what I was going to be doing today, I would have said, "No way, God. That is impossible." I'm so glad that He leads us one step at a time!

You may wonder why you are not very far along in the plan for your life. Let me ask you a question: Are you following God one step at a time? Perhaps you have taken the first step and fallen down. You may still be lying on the ground, having decided to never take another step. Just as a mother encourages her children to get up and try again, so the Heavenly Father is encouraging you to get up and take another step.

We must meet the challenge of each step saying, "Okay, God, with You I will make it this time." I know what it is like to be in fear and trembling, taking that next step in God's plan for your life. The devil will try to do a number on you and whisper in your ear, "You don't think you can accomplish that project, do you?" I talk right back to him and say, "No, Mr. Devil, I don't *think* I can; I *know* I can. It's not me—it's the Lord doing it through me. He's the One Who gave me the assignment. And He would never call me to do anything that He didn't equip me to do. So it's not me—it's God in me."

You have to speak to the devil that way when he is hollering in your ear. If you start taking that attitude in life, you will find that you'll start rising to the top. You will find that opportunities will start knocking on your door. Take advantage of those opportunities with confidence, knowing that with God's wisdom and strength you can do all things.

Psalm 37:23 says, *"The steps of a good man are ordered by the Lord: and he delighteth in his way."* If you will delight in the Lord, He will order your steps—and they will be steps of success and not failure. But when opportunity knocks, answer! You must walk through that door with confidence, knowing you can do it with the help of the Lord.

I love Philippians 4:13 that says, *"I can do all things through Christ which strengtheneth me."* This verse has helped me have confidence in my ability, because I know that I'm not doing anything alone—Christ strengthens me. That verse has also helped me through various disappointments and difficult circumstances in my life.

Sometimes it may seem so dark that you can't see one step ahead. It may be so frightening that you may need to simply close your eyes to the circumstances, grasp the hand of your Heavenly Father, and say, "Father, You said in Your Word that You would never leave me or forsake me. You promised to always be with me. I take Your hand by faith, and I expect You to lead me to victory."

One more thing: We are a time-conscious society. We live such scheduled lives that we want to schedule God's time as well. But His timetable doesn't always match with ours. I'm grateful when He shows me the next step instantly, but I must say that an instant answer or resolution is the exception, not the rule. I used to have difficulty waiting for His direction to unfold. I wanted everything in my timing, *now*. I soon found out that His plan was far superior to mine. In my way and timing, things become catastrophic. God doesn't get in a hurry. He is never early or late; He's always on time.

I want to encourage you that you can make it through every circumstance of your life—regardless of what it is—if you will simply place your hand in God's hand. He will direct your path and lead you to victory . . . one step at a time.

Prayer:

Father, I know now that with You I can make it this time—and every time. I am taking Your hand by faith and expecting You to lead me each step of the way to victory, in Jesus' Name.

Thoughts for the Week:

_____

_____

_____

_____

∕

Spiritual Housecleaning

"First wash the inside of the cup, and then the outside will become clean, too."

Matthew 23:26 NLT

It's a wonderful season when winter gives way to spring. During this time, many people have a tradition of "spring-cleaning" their house. They clean out the closets and throw away things they haven't used in years; and they give a thorough cleaning to other areas of their house that they normally just "surface clean" or clean very quickly. I'm one of those people who considers spring a time to get my house in order. I also feel that perhaps this would be a great time get our spiritual house in order.

You may wonder why your prayers seem to go unanswered. Psalm 37:4–5 says, *"Delight thyself also in the Lord; and he shall give thee the desires of thine heart. Commit thy way unto the Lord; trust also in him; and he shall bring it to pass."* Let me ask you a question: Are you delighting in the Lord? Are you committing your ways to Him? In other words, are you placing God first in your life? That is so important, yet many times we let other things become our top priority. If we are not careful, it is easy to let undesirable things creep into our spiritual house.

One undesirable thing we sometimes allow to creep in is strife. Proverbs 26:21–22 says, *"As coals are to burning coals, and wood to fire; so is a contentious man to kindle strife. The words of a talebearer are as wounds, and they go down into the innermost parts of the belly."* Refuse to allow strife any place in your life or home.

Gossip is also important to get rid of and throw out of our spiritual house. We must not gossip about others. *Talebearer, rumormonger,* and *scandalmonger* are other names for a gossip, and they certainly are not good titles to bear. When someone comes to me and says, "Did you know about So-and-so?" and then talks about that person with destructive words rather than uplifting words, I stop the talebearer in mid-sentence and say, "My ears are not garbage cans; I refuse to listen to anything but uplifting words."

The Apostle Paul told us in Philippians 4:8 to think on things that are true, honest, just, pure, lovely, and of good report. As you choose to think about lovely things, you will find that the bad reports begin to vanish.

You should always choose to look on the positive side of things and refuse to dwell on the negative. When people dwell on the negative, they become miserable and make everyone else around them miserable. But when a person is positive, everyone wants to be in his or her presence.

This spring, as you begin your natural housecleaning, I encourage you to start your spiritual housecleaning as well. Try these "housecleaning" tips. Clean out all the strife and gossip in your life. Clean out negative attitudes you may have toward yourself and others. Pray for a love and compassion for others to encompass you. And most importantly, practice Mark 11:25: *"When ye stand praying, forgive, if ye have ought against any: that your Father also which is in heaven may forgive you your trespasses."*

So many times we quote Mark 11:23–24 concerning the desires of our heart being granted, but we stop short of the very thing that will bring those desires to pass. We must practice the commandment of forgiveness found in verse 25. Often we want forgiveness for ourselves but judgment for everyone else. No, we must forgive if we want forgiveness—and if we want our prayers answered. I've had many opportunities to practice this scripture myself, so I understand that someone might have done an awful thing to you. But I've found that the more you practice verse 25, the easier it becomes. Peace and tranquility will surround you.

You'll watch hatred and bitterness turn to love and forgiveness, and experience a joy like you've never known before.

When I was a child, my parents always quoted Matthew 6:33 to me. It says, *"But seek ye first the kingdom of God, and his righteousness; and all these things shall be added unto you."* It is so important to seek the things of God first and clean out the undesirable things that may have crept into our lives. No matter what time of the year it is, you can commit afresh your ways to God, and watch the desires of your heart be granted.

Prayer:

Father God, I want to get my spiritual house in order. Help me to do a thorough spring cleaning in my mind, will, and emotions and commit afresh my ways to You, in the Name of Jesus.

Thoughts for the Week:

_____

_____

_____

_____

_____

The Mender of Broken Hearts

"He brought me up also out of an horrible pit . . . and he hath
put a new song in my mouth, even praise unto our God."

Psalm 40:2–3

One time I received a letter from a brokenhearted woman
whose 20-year-old daughter went to be with the Lord soon after
having surgery for a cancerous brain tumor. Her daughter had
been a missions major at a Bible college, and a beautiful piano
player and singer. The mother was still in shock over her loss.
Even though she read the Word, prayed, kept busy with family,
and had good Christian friends to talk to, nothing consoled her.
She couldn't understand why God had broken her heart and
taken her daughter so soon in life. And she was having trouble
getting her peace and joy back. I want to share how I answered
her because all of us experience losses at times in our lives.

It takes time for our heart to mend after any kind of loss, especially one of that magnitude. We need to remember that God does not break our heart, nor does He take the person from us. God is not the destroyer; He is the Life-Giver.

According to John 10:10, God sent His Son, Jesus, to redeem us so that we could have life. This same verse identifies who caused that woman's daughter to leave her—the thief who comes to steal, kill, and destroy. First Peter 5:8 tells us that our adversary, our enemy, is the devil and he walks this earth seeking those he may devour.

I don't know why her daughter died as she did, but one thing I do know—God is always on our side. He wants to help us through difficult times. He loves us so much that He sent the precious Holy Spirit to be our Comforter. We need to allow Him to envelop us in His comfort and love, and be our Guide whenever we walk through a time of loss.

We will never forget the loved one or the wonderful times we had together, but the pain those memories bring will begin to ease in time. When the pain does come, often quite unexpectedly, we can concentrate on the good things we enjoyed with the person and remember those wonderful times, instead of thinking about the pain and the hurt of their passing.

You may be struggling with some kind of loss right now. I encourage you to find scriptures about the protection and care of God that speak to you personally. I often go through the Book of Psalms for comfort in various times of need, because I know that David experienced severe losses in his life. And he truly understood the pain that accompanies the death of a child. In several of the psalms, David cried out to God from the depths of pain caused by various circumstances—and God comforted him.

For instance, in Psalm 30:5 David said, *"Weeping may endure for a night, but joy cometh in the morning."* Another time he said in Psalm 38:6, *"I am troubled; I am bowed down greatly; I go mourning all the day long."* Then later in Psalm 40 he said, *"I waited patiently for the Lord; and he inclined unto me, and heard my cry. He brought me up also out of an horrible pit, out of the miry clay, and set my feet upon a rock, and established my goings. And he hath put a new song in my mouth, even praise unto our God"* (vv. 1–3).

You can also experience, just as David did, the joy of realizing that the Lord's mercies are new every morning because of His faithfulness. David knew that his strength and joy came from the Lord, and in his deepest sorrow, he clung to that knowledge. You must also cling to the Lord in various times of need because He is the source of your peace, your strength to endure, and your joy.

Each person and set of circumstances is unique, so I would never attempt to put a timeline on when anyone would begin to experience peace and joy once again. But the good news is, you will.

Prayer:

Father God, You understand the loss of a child better than anyone. You sent Your beloved Son, Jesus, to suffer and die on the cross for our sins. Thank You that when we lose a loved one, You are right there with us to heal our broken hearts, envelop us in Your comfort and love, and restore our peace and joy.

Thoughts for the Week:

WEEK 12

Never Too Busy

"I will always show you where to go. I'll give you a full life in the emptiest of places—firm muscles, strong bones. You'll be like a well-watered garden, a gurgling spring that never runs dry. You'll use the old rubble of past lives to build anew, rebuild the foundations. . . . You'll be known as those who can fix anything, restore old ruins, rebuild and renovate, make the community livable again."

Isaiah 58:11–12 MSG

I am a planner and an organizer. I love to write to-do lists and proudly check off each item during the day. I used to get annoyed by anything that deterred me from my charted path—until the Lord showed me that interruptions are ministry opportunities.

One hectic day I was busy accomplishing a list of errands that I had estimated would take me about four hours to complete. I was on a tight schedule because of other obligations I had to fulfill. As I started with the first project on my list, someone greeted me in the store and then began to pour out her heart and needs to me. I ended up standing in that store for two hours, listening to her hurts.

As I listened I wanted to scream, "I'm too busy for this! I must complete my to-do list!" Then the Lord gently reminded me that this was a ministry opportunity, not an interruption. So I patiently allowed the Holy Spirit to bring forth words of comfort that ministered to her. Because I obeyed, the Lord redeemed my time—the list that should have taken four hours was done in one!

A time-planning expert would have cringed at the way Jesus used His time because He spent it doing things that did not appear to be on His so-called agenda. We see Him detour from His to-do list in Mark 5. Jesus was about to address a crowd when Jairus approached Him and asked Him to come and heal his daughter (v. 23). So Jesus interrupted what He was doing and started to Jairus' house. Of course, the crowd continued to follow Jesus and it was during this time that Jesus was interrupted by the woman with the issue of blood.

That woman seized the moment to get her healing from an issue of blood she had suffered with for 12 years. As the Bible says, she pressed through the crowd in order to reach

Jesus because she believed that when she touched the hem of His garment, she would be healed. And she was because of her touch of faith.

Jesus' disciples were annoyed at this interruption, yet Jesus took time to minister to her anyway: *"He said unto her, Daughter, thy faith hath made thee whole; go in peace, and be whole of thy plague"* (v. 34).

Remember that this interruption happened as Jesus was on His way to heal Jairus' daughter. Soon, word came that the little girl had died, and it appeared that Jesus was too late to heal her because He had taken time to heal the woman with the issue of blood. But Jesus continued on with His mission. And though Jairus' family and friends were already mourning when Jesus and the others arrived, Jesus said to the mourners, *"Why make ye this ado, and weep? the damsel is not dead, but sleepeth"* (v. 39). Jesus then raised Jairus' daughter from the dead.

What if Jesus had refused to help Jairus or minister to the woman with the issue of blood because He had another agenda? How often have we passed up ministry opportunities because we thought of them as interruptions and we were too busy?

I encourage you to stop viewing interruptions as irritations the way I once did, and see them as opportunities. Realize that the Lord may take you down a path of seeming "interruptions" because that path will allow you to minister to the needs of others. When you place people's needs and the plan of God above your own agenda, you will become a blessing and will also be blessed.

Prayer:

Lord, forgive me for the times I've allowed my busyness to cause me to miss out on helping someone who is hurting. I want to always be available to follow You wherever Your path leads. Help me never again to put my agenda ahead of an opportunity to minister to others, in the Name of Jesus.

Thoughts for the Week:

~~

Practicing
the Love Walk

"These things I have spoken to you, that in Me you may have peace."

John 16:33 NKJV

I am shocked at the turmoil that exists in the homes of many Christians. The Lord wants us to live in peace. The Scriptures give us this admonition quite frequently. Yet it seems that peace often does not reign in our lives. For instance, our homes should be places of peace. They should be shelters for us in the midst of troubles in the world. Families should unite together and stand with each other. However, the enemy is playing havoc in the homes of Christians; it is one of his oldest schemes.

The church at Corinth was suffering from such strife within it that the Apostle Paul had to remind the members, *"Be perfect, be of good comfort, be of one mind, live in peace; and the God of love and peace shall be with you"* (2 Cor. 13:11). I believe we should take a hint from Paul's words and adopt the following as our family motto: "Be of one mind. Live in peace."

In order to live out that instruction from Paul, it is important to communicate effectively with others, beginning with your spouse and your children. Communication is often the most difficult skill to master, because you can experience so many different emotions when you are communicating your thoughts and feelings. Paul talked about that in Ephesians 4:26–27: *"Be ye angry, and sin not: let not the sun go down upon your wrath: Neither give place to the devil."* This sounds like a contradictory statement—"be angry and sin not"—but it isn't. The Lord knows that anger is one of the emotions we experience in life, yet He tells us, "Although you may be feeling angry, do not sin." Exactly what does that mean?

I like the way *The Message* Bible explains those verses. It says, *"Go ahead and be angry. You do well to be angry—but don't use your anger as fuel for revenge. And don't stay angry. Don't go to bed angry. Don't give the Devil that kind of foothold in your life."* Yes, you may experience angry feelings, but don't use those feelings to get even. In the midst of anger, you might say words that you may not really mean, but those cutting words will forever ring in the ears of the recipient.

Life is too short to live in constant turmoil in your home. That holds true regarding your relationships with friends and loved ones as well. My husband and I have been married over 42 years, so I can offer you some lessons that I've learned from experience. I believe that following this advice will enhance your marriage journey (it can also be applied to your relationships with others):

- Communicate your feelings and frustrations without getting upset.
- Communicate honestly.
- Choose your words carefully.
- Don't use degrading language. Use words that convey love.
- Communicate with your spouse as you would with a friend.
- Resolve your problems before you go to bed.
- Choose your battles, and overlook minor issues.
- Realize that some things will not change, so accept them.

These are the guidelines that my husband and I have practiced over the years. I will not pretend that they were perfected overnight. But as we began to practice these principles, we found that peace continually reigned in our home. As each of us was willing to readily say, "I'm sorry; forgive me" (words you can say to anyone in your life), the conflict was easily resolved.

I encourage you to start practicing the love walk in your home. Make it a place of comfort and refuge. Don't allow the enemy to bring strife into your life. Recognize the source of that strife and do not give place to it. Make Christ the center of your home. When we place Him first in our homes and marriages, every hostile wall will be broken down and the love of God will rule and reign in our lives.

Prayer:

Father, forgive me for allowing any turmoil, strife, or anger to enter into my home or my other relationships. Help me to quickly resolve every conflict and choose to forgive—even when I don't feel like it—and to start practicing the love walk everywhere I go, in the Name of Jesus.

Thoughts for the Week:

_____

_____

_____

_____

◢

Be a Witness

"God sent not his Son into the world to condemn the world;
but that the world through him might be saved."

John 3:17

During the Easter season, we celebrate the resurrection of
our Lord and Savior. We should remember to thank our Heavenly
Father at Easter and all through the year for sending His Son,
Jesus, to redeem us. I am sure that by now you have seen movies
and heard messages depicting how Jesus suffered on the cross
to accomplish this. Throughout my life I have heard the story
of the Crucifixion told many ways. Listening to my husband
minister on Communion, I've heard the crucifixion described so
vividly that I could mentally picture it. Yet I had not adequately
visualized what agony Jesus went through in dying for our sins
until I saw the movie *The Passion of the Christ*.

Watching it, I was struck by the immense suffering Jesus
endured, and I thought, *What love our God has for us to allow*

His Son to go through such awful pain for people who had failed so miserably. May we all gain a new love and appreciation for what both our Heavenly Father and Jesus did for us so that we might have abundant life.

Many times we take what Christ did for us for granted. We need to be thankful for the sacrifice that He made. Considering what He did in our place, I trust that you will have a great determination, just as I have, to help accomplish the plan of God on this earth. We are God's hands, feet, and voice in this world. Some parts of His plan cannot be accomplished here without us listening to and obeying His instructions.

The end of all things is truly near. Bible prophecy is being fulfilled on a daily basis. Second Timothy 3:1–5 says, *"In the last days perilous times shall come. For men shall be lovers of their own selves, covetous, boasters, proud, blasphemers, disobedient to parents, unthankful, unholy, without natural affection, trucebreakers, false accusers, incontinent, fierce, despisers of those that are good, traitors, heady, highminded, lovers of pleasures more than lovers of God; having a form of godliness, but denying the power thereof: from such turn away."* These scriptures are certainly being fulfilled all around us.

It saddens me to see the condition of our world. It makes me even more determined to be a witness to those who have been deceived by the devil. We should be reaching out to them rather than shunning them. They must be told about the God who loves them so much that He gave His only Son in order that they might have eternal life.

We need to reach out to the lost instead of wrapping our righteous robes around us. We as Christians often forget our real mission—to be a witness for Christ. That means we love people just as our Heavenly Father loves them. He loves us even though we messed up. We must extend that same love, grace, and mercy to the lost and love them into the kingdom—and do the same for other Christians who have made mistakes.

It's a sad indictment, but too often Christians kill their wounded (spiritually speaking). Rather than extending arms of love and mercy, our first instinct is to judge others. Often when a Christian has messed up, we want to judge the person and make statements like, "I can't believe they did that!" The Bible talks about judging others and the consequences: *"Judge not, that ye be not judged"* (Matt. 7:1). Or as *The Message* Bible puts it, *"Don't pick on people, jump on their failures, criticize their faults—unless, of course, you want the same treatment. That critical spirit has a way of boomeranging"* (vv. 1–2 MSG).

Many years ago I adopted the motto, "If I were in the offender's shoes, how would I want to be treated?" We all need to ask ourselves that question and follow that guideline, and watch how our attitudes and judgment err on the side of mercy. Instead of tossing fallen Christians out, we will work to restore them.

God's mercy has truly rewritten each of our lives, and we should extend that same grace toward our brothers and sisters in Christ as well as to the lost. I challenge you today to start finding those who need salvation and restoration and to be instrumental in bringing or restoring those precious people into the sheepfold. That's the true meaning of Easter!

Prayer:

Lord Jesus, thank You for loving me so much that You were willing to suffer and go to the cross to save my soul. Please lead me to those who have not yet received You, and to the fallen, who need to be restored to the sheepfold. Help me share with them Your love, grace, mercy, and gift of salvation.

Thoughts for the Week:

WEEK 15

It Pays to Listen

"To day if ye will hear his voice, harden not your hearts."

Hebrews 3:15

In Oklahoma where I live, many refer to late spring as "storm season." We often hear the local warning siren, alerting us to impending dangerous storms in the area. These storms can quickly evolve into tornadoes that destroy everything in their path.

I can still remember my mother taking me as a young child to our neighbor's storm cellar every time a storm arose. Even if it struck in the middle of the night, my mom would wake me up and take me—sometimes in heavy rain—to find shelter in the cellar built for that very purpose.

The Bible talks about a fierce storm that the Apostle Paul faced in Acts 27. Paul was a prisoner aboard a certain ship that was scheduled to set sail. Because it was a time of year when sailing was dangerous, Paul warned those in command not to leave the harbor, saying, *"Sirs, I perceive that this voyage will be with hurt and much damage, not only of the lading and ship, but also of our lives"* (Acts 27:10). Yet the centurion refused to listen to Paul's advice and continued with the voyage.

A storm indeed arose and the captain and crew began to throw everything overboard in an effort to save the ship. The storm became so treacherous that all hope of being saved was abandoned. Paul came forward and said, *"Men, you should have listened to me, and should not have put to sea from Crete and brought on this disaster and harm and misery and loss. But [even] now I beg you to be in good spirits and take heart, for there will be no loss of life among you but only of the ship. For this [very] night there stood by my side an angel of the God to Whom I belong and Whom I serve and worship, And he said, Do not be frightened, Paul! It is necessary for you to stand before Caesar; and behold, God has given you all those who are sailing with you"* (Acts 27:21–24 AMP).

God often warns His children of impending danger, but some fail to heed His warnings. We would be wise to listen and obey.

When I was a teenager, my friend and I wanted to drive from my home in Texas to her relatives' home in Oklahoma. My father did not want me to go. After I begged him to relent, he reluctantly gave his permission. On the way to Oklahoma, my friend and I encountered a terrible storm. It grew so intense that we couldn't even see the road. Carefully, we pulled over to what we hoped was the side of the road as large hailstones beat against the car. I literally thought that I was going to die.

I did some quick repenting for not listening to my father. Although my friend and I arrived safely at our destination, I learned a good lesson. I should have listened to and obeyed my father—who obviously had been troubled in his spirit about the trip. Since that experience, if I ever feel a check in my spirit when traveling, I always look to the Lord for His direction concerning the matter.

God is concerned about our physical safety. One thing He wants us to do to be protected is to claim His promises on a daily basis. I always claim Psalm 91 for my family: *"There shall no evil befall you, nor any plague or calamity come near your tent. For He will give His angels [especial] charge over you to accompany and defend and preserve you in all your ways [of obedience and service]"* (vv. 10–11 AMP).

I've witnessed God's protecting power many times. Once, we actually heard the sound of a tornado passing over our house. I believe that because we had claimed God's promise of protection for our home, the tornado passed over us without touching down. Several times, the Lord has protected us from car accidents. Once I was going out of town, but something inside of me told me to wait. So I left an hour later. Soon I encountered a traffic jam, and as I came upon the cause of it—a bad accident—I realized that if I had left home when I had first planned, it could have been me in that accident!

I encourage you to call upon the protecting power of God each day. Then be sensitive to His voice, and He will warn you of things to come. If you sense a check in your spirit about something, heed that warning. It pays to listen to the Voice of the Lord.

Prayer:

Father God, thank You for Your protecting power that I can call upon every day. Help me always to listen to You when You warn me of impending dangers, in the Name of Jesus.

Thoughts for the Week:

Walking in God's Perfect Plan

"I know what I'm doing. I have it all planned out—plans to take care of you, not abandon you, plans to give you the future you hope for."

Jeremiah 29:11 MSG

I accepted Christ as my Savior when I was a little girl. While I don't have a testimony of being delivered from drugs or alcohol, I consider my testimony the greatest of all: by the grace of God, I avoided making the choices that would have led me down the wrong path. Even when I was a young child, my heart's desire was to walk in the perfect plan of God for my life.

God has laid it upon my heart to encourage Christians to walk in His perfect will for their life. I have been led to minister along these lines quite a bit, and it is my desire to see the Body of Christ walking in the perfect will of God.

You see, God has a purpose for each one of us. He has a plan for our life. Romans 12:1–2 says, *"I beseech you therefore, brethren, by the mercies of God, that ye present your bodies a living sacrifice, holy, acceptable unto God, which is your reasonable service. And be not conformed to this world: but be ye transformed by the renewing of your mind, that ye may prove what is that good, and acceptable, and perfect, will of God."* This passage tells us that there is a good plan, an acceptable plan, and a perfect plan of God. It is important for us to walk in the perfect will of God.

In order to walk out His plan for me, I have often referred to Proverbs 3:5, which says, *"Trust in the Lord with all thine heart; and lean not unto thine own understanding."* I have made trusting in the Lord a lifelong pattern—and what a difference it has made!

To walk out God's plan for our life, we must put our trust in Him. What does trust mean? One dictionary defines *trust* as a firm belief in the honesty, truthfulness, justice, or power of a person; committed to one's care. It is important that we place our trust in the Lord Jesus Christ. It is important that we commit our lives to His care. When we have a firm belief in God's honesty, truthfulness, justice, and power, we can say, "Father God, I commit my life to You—to be used however You see fit. I want Your will to be my will."

The perfect will of God is different for all of us. He has a specific and special course for each person's life. One thing you can be sure of—it is a course filled with fun, adversity, joy, hard work, and victory. You may have visions, dreams, and goals that you have set for yourself, and they may be what motivate you each day. They may even give you purpose and direction for a time. But only God's purpose for you will bring you the abundant, meaningful life that will take you to the mountaintop.

Trusting the Lord with your life is not an easy task. You may be praying, "Lord, I'll do what You want me to do and go where You want me to go." You may think you are trusting God, but when He asks you to do something that you don't want to do or to go somewhere you don't want to go, then and only then will you discover if you are really trusting the Lord with your life.

When you get to the place of really trusting Him and walking in His perfect will, you can rest in peace—but that doesn't mean that your surroundings will always be peaceful. It does mean that in spite of the circumstances going on around you, you can experience peace because you are resting in the perfect will of God for your life.

If you are going to enjoy a successful and victorious life, you must set aside your own plans, dreams, and desires and trust in the plans, dreams, and desires of the Lord. When you trust in the Lord, He will never lead you down the wrong path. He will lead you from glory to glory and from victory to victory!

Prayer:

Heavenly Father, I want to walk out Your perfect will for my life and put my trust in You. I am setting aside my own desires and plans and trusting in the ones You have for me. Help me to do whatever You ask of me, whether or not it is exactly what I want to do at the time. Thank You that You only have my good in mind and will ultimately bring me into the abundant, meaningful life that You have for me, in the Name of Jesus.

Thoughts for the Week:

⚚

Every Day Can Be Good!

"The mouth of the just bringeth forth wisdom. . . . The lips of the righteous know what is acceptable."

Proverbs 10:31–32

Having a good day doesn't just happen. I believe that it begins with the words you speak when you wake up. That's why it is so important that we start our day with the right kind of words. Psalm 118:24 gives us the right kind of words to say: *"This is the day which the Lord hath made; we will rejoice and be glad in it."* What a good idea to start each day saying what the Bible says!

Now, I know that some people may naturally enjoy getting up early and watching the sunrise—but I'm not one of them. I am just not a morning person. I prefer the night rather than the morning. In fact, my energy level increases around midnight!

It could be challenging for me to say verse 24 before I get out of bed. I'd prefer to say, "Oh, it's morning. I will not rejoice and be glad in it." But I have learned the value of speaking the right kind of words when I arise. So even before my feet hit the floor, I start saying, "This is the day the Lord has made; I will rejoice and be glad in it," because a lot can happen between the time you sit up in bed and when your feet hit the floor!

I remember one morning when I first awoke, I put my foot down on the floor not realizing that my foot was asleep. My foot collapsed beneath me, and I twisted my ankle severely. As I was lying on the floor, gripped with pain, it wasn't easy to say, "This is the day the Lord has made." But as I began to quote that scripture, strength rose up inside of me. I was able to recover from the pain, get up, and perform my tasks for the day.

How important are the words we speak? By our words, we can choose to have a good day or a bad day. Our world is created by the words we speak. I encourage you to start your day by boldly making your confessions of faith.

For example, each day I have certain things for which I ask the Lord. First, I ask Him for *wisdom*. James 1:5 says, *"If any of you lack wisdom, let him ask of God, that giveth to all men liberally, and upbraideth not; and it shall be given him."* I have found that as

I ask for wisdom, the Lord helps me in making major decisions as well as daily minor decisions. I have often seen people stress over making decisions. I simply tell them that the Word says we have not because we ask not (James 4:2), and if they would ask the Lord for wisdom, decisions could be made more quickly.

The Lord is always ready to assist us in anything that we need. Yet, it seems we neglect to ask of Him until we have exhausted every other avenue. Why not try going to the Lord first? We will find that we will save a lot of time and effort.

Another thing that I ask for daily is *strength*. Isaiah 40:31 tells us, *"But they that wait upon the Lord shall renew their strength; they shall mount up with wings as eagles; they shall run, and not be weary; and they shall walk, and not faint."* As I wait upon the Lord and commune with Him, He does renew my strength. People often say to me, "You are so full of energy. What is your secret? Do you take vitamins?" I tell them, "It's not vitamins. I simply ask the Lord to supply me with an abundance of energy. And He always accommodates me."

The Word also says that a merry heart does us good like a medicine (Prov. 17:22), and that the joy of the Lord is our strength (Neh. 8:10). So if I'm getting stressed out, I begin to laugh. I find that as I laugh, my stress disappears and my strength is renewed.

Whatever circumstances you may be encountering today, know that the Heavenly Father cares about you. Your circumstances may look bleak, but those circumstances can be changed when you speak the Word of God. Choose to have a good day; say you will have a good day; and watch your good day become a reality!

Prayer:

Father, thank You for Your Word that can change our circumstances when we speak it. In the Name of Jesus, help me to start each day by filling my mouth with the Word and boldly making my confessions of faith, beginning with this: I am going to have a good day today!

Thoughts for the Week:

∽

No One Is an Island

"If we love one another, God lives in us and his love is made complete in us."

1 John 4:12 NIV

I remember an incident that occurred in my life when I was a child. I was hurt very deeply by a person with whom I had spent much time developing a relationship. My father was comforting me and in the midst of my hurt, I said to him, "I'm never going to have another friend. The hurt is too deep. I am just going to live my life to myself."

His words of wisdom still ring in my ears: "Lynette, you are a giving person. You would not be happy if you were not giving of yourself to others. Remember, the hurt will pass and you will find another friend." Although at that moment, I didn't want to receive his advice, I knew he was right. I would be miserable if I were not giving of myself to others. I'm so thankful that my parents taught me the importance of developing relationships and

I didn't end up living my life the way I had told my father that day. I often heard the phase "no man is an island" during my childhood, and it is so true! All of us would experience an awfully lonely life if we did not share ourselves with others. We do need other people, and they need us as well. No doubt you have had the opportunity to say, "If it weren't for people, my life would be wonderful." But the truth is we all need each other. If you are skeptical, find someone who is self-centered and never imparts of their time or talent to others and you will see a miserable and unhappy person.

Regardless of the kind of relationship (friendships or parents and children or siblings or spouses, for example), the act of giving and receiving is a very important part of relationships that none of us can do without. Yet in the times in which we live, many people seem to have lost sight of the importance of relationships or how to develop them.

Of course, the most important person we need to develop a relationship with is God. In Matthew 22:37 Jesus said these words, *"Thou shalt love the Lord thy God with all thy heart, and with all thy soul, and with all thy mind."* I'm sure you agree that you cannot love someone with whom you have not established a relationship.

God does not have any grandchildren. Each one of us must develop our individual relationship with Christ. If you have not accepted Jesus Christ as your Savior, I encourage you to do so right now. Pray the prayer for salvation that you will find at the back of this book. Don't wait another day. Jesus loved you so much that He gave His very life so that you might have eternal life. Receive Him as your Lord and Savior today; then get to know Him personally. (Read His Word and talk to Him daily!)

Another relationship we must nurture is with our parents. Exodus 20:12 says, *"Honor your father and mother. Then you will live a long, full life in the land . . . God is giving you"* (NLT). This is the first commandment with promise—God said that if we honor our father and mother, He will give us a long life. I was often reminded of this as a child, especially when I was being disobedient. But I am so glad that my parents instilled that principle in me. Even after I was grown, I endeavored to honor and respect them.

As you honor your parents, it is important to develop a relationship with them. You may be thinking, *My parents really annoy me.* Have you ever thought that the reason for that is, you may possess a lot of their characteristics? I have found that as you mature, unconsciously you will develop some of the same habits as your parents. Some may be good—some may not be so good. Strive to enhance those good characteristics from your parents and delete the annoying ones. But always be considerate of your parents. Treat them the way you would like to be treated at their age. I think it's important to plant good seeds for your future.

So the act of giving and receiving in any good relationship involves attitude and action. There comes a time when words and thoughts have to be followed up with consistent actions and deeds—acts of kindness are one of the strongest voices in relationships. I encourage you to nurture the relationships you already have and begin to develop new ones—it is a key to living a fulfilled life.

Prayer:

Dear Lord, thank You for creating us to be social. Help me never to forget to lovingly nurture and tenderly develop relationships with people You place in my life. And give me the wisdom to do it, in Jesus' Name.

Thoughts for the Week:

_____

_____

_____

_____

🌿

Live Worry-Free

"Do not fret or have any anxiety about anything, but in every circumstance and in everything, by prayer and petition (definite requests), with thanksgiving, continue to make your wants known to God."

Philippians 4:6 AMP

Worry is something we all have faced. We may love the Lord with all our heart, yet still have a problem with worrying that we can't seem to get over. The reason may be that every time we think we're free from worrying, the devil is there to throw something in our face. He continually tries to tempt us in this area. When we allow worry to dominate us, fear is right there waiting to become a stronghold in our life. But we can be free from worry!

I used to be a world-champion worrier. I worried about everything. Fear and worry dominated my life. Yes, I had heard ministers preach on worrying. They admonished the congregation on the importance of winning the battle over worry, and I readily agreed with them. But having knowledge of something and being able to live it out in my own life were two different things.

I soon realized that if I didn't take control of worry and fear, they would take control of me—for the rest of my life! Not only would I be miserable, but the stress caused by worry and fear would eventually break me down emotionally and physically. So I began to search the Word of God for myself, looking for answers. You see, inspiration may come and go. Feelings may come and go. My friends may be there to encourage me one day and then not be available another. But the Word of God is always there with the answers to all of my needs. (That's one reason the Bible has become so precious to me.)

To find the solution to my worrying problem I went to the Bible. Some of the scriptures I found on worry include Philippians 4:6 that says, *"Do not fret or have any anxiety about anything, but in every circumstance and in everything, by prayer and petition (definite requests), with thanksgiving, continue to make your wants known to God"* (AMP). Another verse that was quickened to my spirit was 1 Peter 5:7, which says, *"Casting the whole of your care [all your anxieties, all your worries, all your concerns, once and for all] on Him, for He cares for you affectionately and cares about you watchfully"* (AMP). And the words of Psalm 55:22 comforted me: *"Cast your burden on the Lord [releasing the weight of it] and He will sustain you; He will never allow the [consistently] righteous to be moved (made to slip, fall, or fail)"* (AMP).

As I began to read these scriptures, I realized that although I loved the Lord with all my heart, I had not wholly put my trust in Him and in His promises. Imagine a parent saying to his child, "I promise to take good care of you. I will feed you, clothe you, and make sure that all of your needs are met." After a child has heard his parent make that promise, it would be ridiculous for him to continue to worry that he may starve to death, that his clothes may wear out, or that his other needs may not be met. No, when a parent says, "I will do such and such," the child doesn't give it a second thought. He believes that what his parent has said shall indeed be done.

Suddenly, I realized how grieved my Heavenly Father must have been by my continually worrying about the very things He had promised me in His Word. I had let fear dominate my life instead of trusting my Heavenly Father Whom I loved so much.

At that time, I made a quality decision that I was no longer going to let the devil steal my confidence in the Lord. I began to trust the One Who promised me in His Word that He would take care of me and supply all of my needs.

I also made a quality decision to turn to the Word of God when faced with a concern in life—to find a promise of God that met my specific need. I encourage you to do the same thing, and you will find that you can live a life free of worry and fear.

Prayer:

Father God, forgive me for letting fear dominate my life instead of trusting in You. I know that You have the answers to all my needs and from now on I am going to hang up my worries, cast my cares upon You, and wholly rest in Your promises, in the Name of Jesus.

Thoughts for the Week:

⌒

'Honor Thy Mother'

"Honour thy father and thy mother: that thy days may be long upon the land which the Lord thy God giveth thee."

Exodus 20:12

In May of each year, Americans set aside one Sunday to honor mothers. This holiday is actually biblical—Exodus 20:12 commands us to honor our mothers and we'll live a long life. That day is very special to me for a couple of other reasons: I was born on Mother's Day (so I feel special because of that significance), and I am a mother (so it's a time when my children honor me).

It is a very rewarding feeling to receive beautiful Mother's Day cards from my children—cards expressing true sentiments that aren't always verbalized. In the hustle and bustle of life, we often fail to honor the one to whom we owe our life.

Mothers have been given a powerful responsibility to birth, nurture, and train their children . . . and then learn to let go of them. Mothers make many sacrifices in raising us. It has been said that a man's work is from sun to sun, but a woman's work is never done. At times, mothers find it difficult to balance all their tasks. Yet when we were children, mother was always there. She was there to tend to us when we were sick. And if she could have taken our place, she would have. My mother always made potato soup for us when we were sick. That in itself seemed to begin the healing process. We knew that Mother's soup would do wonders for us!

I think it is important for us to continue to honor our parents even after we are adults and to let them know how much we appreciate all they have provided for us. Abraham Lincoln once said, "All that I am or ever hope to be, I owe to my angel mother." George Washington put it this way: "My mother was the most beautiful woman I ever saw. All I am, I owe to my mother. I attribute all my success in life to the moral, intellectual, and physical education I received from her."

As we grow older and have our own children, we realize what an awesome responsibility motherhood is. We realize that the natural things we do for our children are important, and they will be cherished memories. But the most important contribution we can give to our children is a heritage of faith in the Lord.

Paul, in writing to Timothy, said it like this: *"I have been reminded of your sincere faith, which first lived in your grandmother Lois and in your mother Eunice and, I am persuaded, now lives in you also"* (2 Tim. 1:5 NIV). These women not only lived their faith, but they passed it on to Timothy. They realized that it was their responsibility to teach Timothy about the things of God and to be a daily example for him to follow.

I am so thankful for the heritage of faith and the spiritual example that I received from my mother. I would daily see her commune with God in the Word, as well as in prayer. When things would get tough, she knew that God would take care of it for her. The things of God were always first place in our home. She taught me how to be a godly wife. I observed her always standing beside my father in ministry, supporting him in every way. Her example has made me what I am today—standing beside my husband and together carrying out God's plan for our lives. I am forever grateful for the foundation I received from her. It gave me the strength to withstand the trials and adversities of life.

Your own mother may have been a very strong person and you might wonder, *Can I ever fit into her shoes?* No, we wear our own shoes. You may never do things exactly as she did. But if you came from a Christian home as I did, she has given you the pattern upon which to build—to bring up your children in the ways of the Lord (Prov. 22:6). If you weren't brought up in a Christian home, make the decision today that you will begin that godly pattern for your children to follow in raising their children.

So I encourage you to remember your mother on Mother's Day. Send her a card or call her on her special day to thank her for the good things she has done for you. And if your mother has already gone on to be with the Lord, I encourage you to take a moment to thank God for her and to remember the great memories you have of her time with you.

Prayer:

Thank You, Lord, for my mother and for the part she had in making me who I am today. Help me to build upon that and follow Your wisdom to make my home one that is good, happy, and Christ-honoring, in Jesus' Name.

Thoughts for the Week:

Fear Not!

"For God hath not given us the spirit of fear; but of power, and of love, and of a sound mind."

2 Timothy 1:7

I remember as a child going to my grandmother's house and listening to her tell me stories, which I called, "I remember when." All the grandchildren loved to hear her fascinating tales about life without cars, electricity, indoor bathrooms, and so forth. We couldn't imagine life without some of the things she did not have when she was young.

Now I find myself in the same position. I'm able to tell my grandchildren my own "I remember when" stories about life without color television, remote controls, computers, cell phones, and the like when I was growing up. I can remember visiting some of the larger amusement parks with Ken and our children, and seeing exhibits that introduced you to the inventions of tomorrow. Sometimes we could hardly fathom that those things would become a reality, and yet presently we are living with that technology.

One of the things that stood out in my childhood was that it was unnecessary to lock your house. Very seldom did you hear of burglaries in the neighborhood. It wasn't until the 1970s that I began locking my car. Theft was not a part of our thought patterns, but times certainly have changed. In this day of violence and crime happening on a regular basis, it seems essential not only to lock our possessions but also to install security systems. They have become commonplace commodity.

If we're not careful, it's very easy to allow fear to dominate our lives. We need to remember that we're living in the last days. Second Timothy 3:1–4 says, *"There will be terrible times in the last days. People will be lovers of themselves, lovers of money, boastful, proud, abusive, disobedient to their parents, ungrateful, unholy, without love, unforgiving, slanderous, without self-control, brutal, not lovers of the good, treacherous, rash, conceited, lovers of pleasure rather than lovers of God"* (NIV).

It is easy to become fearful and distraught in these times, but Jesus instructed us about the last days, *"When ye shall hear of wars and commotions, be not terrified . . . "* (Luke 21:9). Fear is an automatic reaction in the natural realm. I believe that is why we're told so often in the Word, "Fear not." It seems that we need to constantly be reminded that we do not have to fear when we are walking under the protective hand of God.

I can still hear my father-in-law say: "Faith and fear cannot reside together. If you are full of fear, you are not in faith." Fear is a spirit. Second Timothy 1:7 says, *"God hath not given us the spirit of fear; but of power, and of love, and of a sound mind."* The enemy would love for fear to dominate our lives. Fear can actually create physical symptoms in our body. Fear can affect our emotional well–being. Fear can paralyze us.

I admonish you to recognize that fear does not come from God; it comes from the devil. When the enemy brings fearful thoughts to you, combat those thoughts with the Word of God. When fear tries to attack me, I immediately quote Isaiah 26:3, *"Thou wilt keep him in perfect peace, whose mind is stayed on thee: because he trusteth in thee."*

My grandsons were not fearful of jumping off of our platform at church when they were younger because they knew their Poppy would be there to catch them. It is important for us to realize that our Heavenly Father is always there to catch us in His arms when the circumstances of life try to cave in on us.

When the doctor gives you a gloomy report, you don't have to fear. Instead, quote Psalm 118:17, *"I shall not die, but live, and* declare the works of the Lord." If you are going through tough circumstances, look to Isaiah 43:2 for strength: *"When thou passest through the waters, I will be with thee; and through the rivers, they shall not overflow thee: when thou walkest through the fire, thou shalt not be burned; neither shall the flame kindle upon thee."* When your budget won't balance, quote Philippians 4:19: *"My God shall supply all your need according to his riches in glory by Christ Jesus"* (NKJV).

You can live your life in faith instead of fear when you place your trust in God!

Prayer:

Father God, I am placing my trust in You. From now on I am going to live my life in faith, not fear, knowing that I am always walking under Your protective hand, in the Name of Jesus.

Thoughts for the Week:

_____

_____

_____

_____

WEEK 22

God Answers Prayer

"We're watching and waiting, holding our breath, awaiting your word of mercy."

Psalm 123:2 MSG

When we are faced with a disturbing situation or one for which we need guidance, our tendency is to concentrate on the situation so much, endeavoring to handle it ourselves, that we don't listen to the inward man, our spirit man. Our mind, the soulish part of us, is so busy trying to solve the problem, we are often unable to hear the still, small voice in our spirit. We need to empty our minds, get quiet, and wait on the Lord.

This confuses some people because they don't know how to do that without emptying their minds of all thoughts as taught in Eastern meditation. Whenever I advise people to quiet or empty their mind and wait on the Lord, I'm not talking about something done in some kind of false religion. Quieting our mind means that we begin meditating on the things of God instead of on the situation around us.

The Word of God admonishes us to keep our mind on Jesus, instead of on the problem. Isaiah 26:3 says, *"Thou wilt keep him in perfect peace, whose mind is stayed on thee: because he trusteth in thee."* We all need perfect peace for the days in which we are living. And we all need answers to certain problems or situations we face in life. God speaks to each person's heart in various ways.

When I need an answer in my life, I often find the answer in the Word of God. As I read the Bible, the Lord will show me something in a particular scripture that I had not seen—even though I may have read that verse many times before. Contained in that scripture is the solution to my problem, or direction for my life.

At other times, the Lord speaks to me through prayer. As I pray about a certain situation, the Lord will often drop the answer into my spirit—an answer that I had not even considered until then. Many times, I do not receive an answer the very instant I pray. It may come several days later, when I am not even thinking about it. I may be doing something as natural as getting ready in the morning or driving in my car, and suddenly the answer comes from the Lord.

God has also used people to provide answers to what I've been praying about. Once I was praying about filling a job vacancy in our ministry. I didn't tell anyone about it, but instead asked God for the right replacement. In talking with a member of our staff some time after I prayed, the person suddenly said to me, "By the way, I just talked to So-and-so. He said that if a vacancy ever occurs, he desires to work for the ministry." Little did that person know he had been used by God to deliver a message for which I had been praying.

God always answers prayer! But He uses a variety of ways to speak to us. When you wait on the Lord, you may hear Him:

- through reading the Bible
- through prayer
- through other people
- through a child
- through a situation
- through an open door of opportunity, or through a closed door of opportunity.

The most important thing is that you are sensitive to know when He is speaking.

I encourage you to learn to wait upon the Lord to reveal the answers you need in the many situations of your life.

My father-in-law (Kenneth E. Hagin) is a fine example of someone who did not make a move until he waited on God to give him specific directions. And I think one of the reasons David was called a man after God's own heart was because he knew the value of waiting on God for the answers he needed. (See Ps. 27:14.)

When you simply go to God and ask for His guidance, you can rest with confidence that He will answer. The key is to trust Him and keep your mind stayed on Him. The answer may not come in your time frame, but it will always come—in God's perfect way and time.

Prayer:

Lord, forgive me for trying to handle my problems myself. Thank You that You are bringing me the answers I need as I quiet my mind and wait on You for Your directions, in the Name of Jesus.

Thoughts for the Week:

_____

_____

_____

_____

_____

Living Happily Ever After

"Wives, be subject (be submissive and adapt yourselves) to your own husbands as [a service] to the Lord. . . . Husbands, love your wives, as Christ loved the church and gave Himself up for her."

Ephesians 5:22, 25 AMP

I always think of weddings whenever I think of the month of June. The reason is that many women choose to become "June brides." But regardless of what time of year a couple "tie the knot," every bride and groom probably envision a storybook marriage. When the minister asks, "Do you take this man/woman to be your lawfully wedded husband/wife?" we all answer, "I do," believing that we will live happily ever after. Unfortunately, the "living happily ever after" takes more work than most of us ever imagined!

Every time my husband and I perform a wedding, my mind is flooded with memories of our own wedding, which took place over 42 years ago. Unfortunately, the only premarital counseling or advice we received was, "If you love each other, just get married and then work out all of your problems." We quickly found that advice to be insufficient.

We weren't advised on how to work out our problems, and we had to learn by trial and error. But we discovered one of the greatest keys to wedded bliss—developing a strong system of communication. When we learned to express our feelings or frustrations in an assertive manner (with healing words) rather than an aggressive one (with hurtful words), our lines of communication began to open.

The Bible tells us to *"Let no corrupt communication proceed out of your mouth, but that which is good to the use of edifying, that it may minister grace unto the hearers"* (Eph. 4:29). When communicating, our goal should always be to *build up (edify) our spouse*, not tear him or her down.

For instance, if a husband comes home to an unkempt house and he's frustrated by it, he has a choice. He can aggressively express his feelings by saying, "You are a lousy housekeeper," and hurt his wife, causing her to become defensive and retaliate. Or he can choose to use healing words rather than hurtful ones by saying, "Honey, I like the house to be clean when I come home. It really frustrates me when it is not clean." Using "I" and "me" words better express how we feel, while "you" words are accusatory and can hurt our spouse. This is easier said than done and can take many years to accomplish, but it's worth the effort.

Truly listening to each other is another communication skill to work at achieving. True listening means that instead of thinking about how we are going to respond while our spouse is still talking, we are concentrating on what our spouse is saying so we can interpret it accurately. Sometimes true listening—and understanding— can be quite a chore because men and women use different communication methods.

Generally, women communicate with their emotions and feelings. They want to have heart-to-heart talks and are interested in details. Men tend to be more analytical and logical and want to get to the bottom line. A healthy marriage requires both the husband and the wife to be flexible in these areas. When each partner gives, there is neither a winner nor a loser—both win.

While communication is a vital necessity to a happy marriage, above all, husbands and wives must both make Jesus the Lord of their lives and of the home. When we do, everything else—including our communication skills—can prosper and we truly can live happily ever after!

Prayer:

Father God, I don't want things to be done only my way in my marriage anymore. Help me to be flexible with my spouse, to place giving above receiving, and always to communicate in a loving, caring, edifying way, in the Name of Jesus.

Thoughts for the Week:

Forgive and Forget

"Like an athlete I . . . [am] training [my body] to do what it
should, not what it wants to."

1 Corinthians 9:27 TLB

In our daily Bible reading, most of us are prone to go to the
passages of Scripture that encourage us, strengthen us, and build
our faith in the Word of God. This is all well and good, but God
knows that we all must deal with our human nature too. So His
Word also commands us to do things our carnal nature wants to
continually ignore. One thing our carnal nature would rather do
is get even, instead of forgiving someone who hurts us.

I had to deal with that many years ago. The Lord had indel-
ibly impressed upon me that if I wanted His promises to work in
my life, I was going to have to heed Matthew 5:44. The problem
was that Matthew 5:44 was a scripture I wanted to ignore. In
it Jesus said, *"Love your enemies, bless them that curse you, do*

good to them that hate you, and pray for them which despitefully use you, and persecute you." I wanted to interpret that scripture this way: "Have nothing to do with your enemies, talk about them who curse you, do evil to them who hate you, and pray for God's wrath to come upon those who despitefully use you, and persecute you."

I realized that loving my enemies, blessing them, and praying for them was not a thing that I naturally wanted to do. I didn't want to hate them; I just wanted to ignore the fact that they existed. As far as I was concerned, I wanted to write them out of my life and I wrestled with this scripture and my carnal feelings. Finally the Lord said to me, "Lynette, I want Matthew 5:44 to be the first scripture you read in your daily devotions. You read that scripture until you can truly begin loving that person who has hurt you the most, and until you can bless them and pray for them without your humanity rebelling."

Maybe you don't have difficulty in this area, but I have to be honest with you. It took me several months of reading this scripture daily to be able to put it into practice without feeling resentment. So many times, the hurt we experience from our enemies cuts so deeply into our emotions that we become prisoners of that wound, especially when the hurt comes from a close friend and turns them into a bitter enemy. That can wound so deeply that instead of releasing forgiveness, we allow the seed of bitterness to creep in.

The writer of Hebrews talked about bitterness, saying, *"Look after each other so that not one of you will fail to find God's best blessings. Watch out that no bitterness takes root among you, for as it springs up it causes deep trouble, hurting many in their spiritual lives"* (Heb. 12:15 TLB). You see, bitterness can grow a little at a time until it becomes so overwhelming that it dominates our entire life.

Have you ever known a bitter person? I have talked with some people who always speak derogatorily about everyone. In fact, when I left their presence, I felt as though I needed to take a shower because of all their vile remarks. But Paul admonishes us in Philippians 4:8, *"Finally, brethren, whatsoever things are true . . . honest . . . just . . . pure . . . lovely . . . [and] of good report; if there be any virtue, and if there be any praise, think on these things."* Jesus' statement in Matthew 12:34 tells us why what we think is important: *"Out of the abundance of the heart [your thoughts] the mouth speaks"* (Matt. 12:34 NKJV).

I always endeavor to concentrate on the *good reports*. Find something good to say about everyone—and that means your enemies as well. If you have had trouble forgiving someone who has hurt you, I encourage you to do as I did. Read Matthew 5:44 every day until it becomes a reality in your life.

Remember that you are only harming yourself when you let the wounds of hurts dominate your life. Forget the hurts; forgive those who have wronged you and pray for them. Your future does not depend upon what someone does or says about you, but upon what God has promised you. Focus on His promises!

Prayer:

Lord, there are people who have deeply hurt and wounded my heart, and it has been difficult for me to forgive them and forget the hurts. Help me to forgive as You have forgiven me. I want to pray for them and let go of the anger and bitterness I've held in my heart so I can be filled with the joy and peace that You want me to experience, in the Name of Jesus.

Thoughts for the Week:

_____

_____

_____

_____

Stand Strong

"We are assured and know that [God being a partner in their labor] all things work together and are [fitting into a plan] for good to and for those who love God and are called according to [His] design and purpose."

Romans 8:28 AMP

I don't think I have ever seen as much stress and as many struggles among Christians as I see at this present time. It seems that the enemy is having a heyday. In some instances, he is successfully destroying Christians or causing them to live defeated lives. The intensity of his onslaught has caused some Christians to give up their fight of faith and say it's not worth it. Yet giving up and being defeated is not the plan of God for our life.

Although the Bible tells us in Romans 8:28, *"All things work together for good to them that love God,"* you might be thinking, *All things are not working together for good for me right now!* It may seem that way, but Jeremiah 29:11 says that God has a plan for your life, and His plan is good: *"'For I know the plans I have for you,' says the Lord. 'They are plans for good and not for disaster, to give you a future and a hope'"* (NLT). The truth is, God had a good plan for your life from the very moment you were created—but the success of that plan depends upon how well you follow His will for you and walk it out.

Psalm 37:23 talks about following God, saying *"The steps of a [good] man are directed and established by the Lord when He delights in his way [and He busies Himself with his every step]"* (AMP). The problem is that many Christians seem to be deceived and think that if they are following the will of God and He is directing their steps, the road of life will be easy and problem-free. They often use having or not having problems as the gauge to determine whether they are in God's will. They think that *not* having any problems means they are in the will of God—but most of the time, it is the other way around.

When you allow your steps to be directed of the Lord and determine that you are going to follow His will for your life, the devil is going to show up. He's going to try to stop you from fulfilling the will of God. Here's the reason why. The devil knows that a believer who is filled with the Holy Spirit, who is full of the Word of God, and who speaks the Name of Jesus is dangerous to him. The devil knows that this kind of person is going to make a difference in the Kingdom of God.

If you are that kind of believer, the devil knows that you are going to tear his evil kingdom down—which means you are a threat to him. What do we try to do to the things that are a threat to us? We try to destroy them! And that's what the devil is trying to do to you. He wants to destroy you!

You must realize that facing battles in life doesn't mean you are out of the will of God. And, regardless of how things look in the natural, you must believe that the path that God has planned for your life will work for your good.

So be encouraged! Psalm 34:19 says, *"Many are the afflictions of the righteous: but the Lord delivereth him out of them all."* No matter what problems you are facing, no matter what the devil may try to do to you, God promises that He will deliver you! Victory will come! Just stand strong (Eph. 6:13) and don't quit following His plan for your life! As Galatians 6:9 says, *"Let us not be weary in well doing: for in due season we shall reap, if we faint not."*

You may feel like giving up "the good fight of faith" (1 Tim. 6:12), but let me encourage you today. Don't let the devil steal your joy. Trust in the Lord. Let Him guide you one step at a time. And know that He will work all things for good to those who love Him.

Prayer:

Heavenly Father, thank You for creating me with a specific plan in mind, and for guiding me each step along the way to fulfilling it. When the road of life gets tough, I will not get weary and quit; I will continue on in You and stand strong, trusting You to deliver me and give me the victory, in the Name of Jesus

Thoughts for the Week:

The Way to Win

"If any of you lack wisdom, let him ask of God, that giveth to all men liberally . . . and it shall be given him."

James 1:5

Keeping a positive attitude is another key to walking out God's plan for your life. A negative attitude will prevent you from reaching the destination that God has planned for you, but a positive attitude will help push you forward—even when obstacles or detours seem to block your path.

My father always possessed a positive attitude in life and he wanted me to have one too. So he often gave me articles to read about attitudes, but one of them really impacted me, even more than the others. These are the truths it contained:

- The *loser* is always part of the problem; the *winner* is always part of the answer.
- The *loser* always has an excuse; the *winner* always has a goal.

- The *loser* says, "That's not my job." The *winner* says, "Let me do it for you."
- The *loser* sees a problem for every answer; the *winner* sees an answer for every problem.
- The *loser* sees two or three sand traps near every green; the *winner* sees a green near every sand trap.
- The *loser* says, "It may be possible, but it's too difficult." The *winner* says, "It may be difficult, but it's possible."

You can see from this list that it takes adopting a winner's attitude to be a success in life. To be a winner, you must take the attitude that believes and declares, "I have the ability to accomplish the plan of God for my life, and with the help of the Lord, I will follow that plan to completion."

My dad always told me, "Lynette, with the help of the Lord, there isn't anything you can't do." The words "I can't" were never allowed to be a part of my vocabulary. I suppose that is why I found Philippians 4:13 at an early age—I had to! That verse has been a means of survival for me. I've quoted many times in my life, "I can do all things through Christ who strengthens me" when in the natural it didn't look like I could!

I also learned James 1:5 early in life: *"If any of you lack wisdom, let him ask of God, that giveth to all men liberally."* I knew that if "I can't" could not be in my vocabulary, I not only needed the strength of the Lord, but also His wisdom! With the strength and wisdom of God, you can accomplish all that He desires you to accomplish.

You may be thinking, *But I feel so inadequate in my job. I'm not going to be promoted, because I don't have the proper education or training that I need.* Or perhaps you have been placed in a position and you are stressed because you're thinking, *I don't have the knowledge or the ability or the personality that it takes to perform the tasks that have been assigned to me.* Who says you don't? Remember, God says you can do all things through Him. Stop thinking of yourself with an "I can't" mentality, and start thinking of yourself with an "I can!" one. Say, "I can be a success in Christ. I can be promoted. I can have favor with my employer. I can do what I've been assigned to do."

Soon after I was married, the company that I worked for closed down. I searched for another job and finally interviewed for a position that required experience on a certain type of calculating machine. During the interview, I was asked about my experience. I replied, "Sir, I am excellent in math (that was a fact), but I don't have experience on the machine that is required for this position." Then I backed up that truth with my words of faith: "But I believe I can do the job." My confidence was not in myself, but in the help and wisdom of the Lord. The man hired me above those who had experience because I displayed confidence in my ability. Of course, my confidence wasn't in what *I* could do, but in what God could do through me if I would rely on His strength and wisdom.

Relying on the strength and wisdom of God is the only way to win in life. So I encourage you to do just that! Rely on His strength and wisdom in every area of your life. Keep a positive attitude. Speak the Word of God over yourself on a daily basis. And the Lord will give you the ability to carry out the plan He has destined for your life.

Prayer:

Lord, let me never assume that I can win in life without relying on the ability You give me to do so. Remind me to look to You for wisdom and strength in all that I do each day, in the Name of Jesus.

Thoughts for the Week:

~

God Can Turn It Around

"Train up a child in the way he should go: and when he is old, he will not depart from it."

Proverbs 22:6

Helping people has always been a great joy to me. I especially desire to help parents (and legal guardians) because many face such tremendous challenges with child rearing nowadays. I receive so many letters from parents who are going through struggles in that area, but I'll never forget the letter from one particular mother who felt she had failed because her grown son had drifted away from God. In my answer, I led her to the Word and how to apply it to her situation.

I sense the Lord impressing me to share this letter and my reply with you. Even if you aren't raising children yourself, I encourage you to apply these biblical principles to any troubled relationship in which you are involved or to any family member or other loved one who is away from the Lord. He can turn the situation around.

Q. *I have a son who is 24 years old. I am writing because I feel I have failed him. I am a Christian, and I took him to church regularly when he was younger. When he was in grade school, he began going to church with his grandma because a lot of his class-mates attended her church. He received salvation at Vacation Bible School. As a teenager, he didn't go to church as much. My son seems to be angry, resentful, and harsh, and he also uses foul language. I feel I failed him because I did not pray or teach him at home like I should have. I look back with such regret. Do you have scriptures I could pray over my son? How should I approach God in prayer concerning these issues?*

A. Looking back, you may now be able to see things that you could have done differently. We all learn as we grow in the Lord. As you go to God in prayer, search your heart, and if you see that you missed it somewhere, ask the Lord to forgive you. He is full of mercy and compassion, and His Word says that He will forgive you.

The important thing is to talk to the Lord about your son. Talking to your son at this point may not be the best thing, especially if he is angry and resentful toward you. So talk to God about the situation, and walk in love toward your son. Many times I heard my father-in-law tell parents who were concerned about their children's spiritual condition to simply surround them with faith and love. Have faith that your son will return to the things of God and love him in spite of his current condition with the Lord.

If there is anything you know you might have done to offend your son, something that he feels he has reason to be angry about, apologize and ask him to forgive you. Even if he refuses your gesture, your love and humility toward him will go a long way toward softening his heart. Proverbs 15:1 says that a gentle answer turns away wrath.

You can also pray that laborers will come across your son's path—people who will witness to him, people he will receive from. I have found that someone outside the family can often be a more effective witness than a family member can be.

Keep in mind that no matter what you do (and even if you did everything right years ago), your son is free to exercise his own will in deciding whether to live for God. But Proverbs 22:6 does say that if you train your child in the way he should go, when he is old, he will not depart from it. You did train your son as a child, taking him to church and sending him to church with his grandma. So you can stand on that verse, believing that your son will return to that which he knew as a child.

Make that your confession: "My son knows the Lord. My son has accepted Jesus as his Savior. And, God, Your Word says that it's Your kindness that leads people to repentance. So I thank You that right now that You are drawing my son back to You. I thank You that my son will live for You and serve you all the days of his life."

I also encourage you to pray over your son the prayers that Paul prayed for the churches: Ephesians 1:15–23; 3:14–21; Colossians 1:9–14; and Philippians 1:9–11. And I encourage you to stand on the following scriptures for yourself: Isaiah 26:3; Philippians 4:6–7; and Romans 14:17–19.

Prayer:

Heavenly Father, forgive me for missing it at times with my child. Thank You for Your Word and Your timeless wisdom that not only can draw my child to You but also can improve our relationship with each other, in the Name of Jesus.

Thoughts for the Week:

◠

A Word in Due Season

"The Lord will guide you always: he will satisfy your needs in a sun-scorched land and will strengthen your frame. . . ."

Isaiah 58:11 NIV

A word spoken in due season can have such a dramatic effect on a life. I want to share two more questions that were submitted to me by people facing difficult situations, followed by my answers sowed into their lives. I believe that these will help and encourage you no matter what you may be facing.

Q. *You have said that you were called into the ministry as a young child. How did you know when it was time to enter your ministry? What sign did God give you? I went to a church-sponsored prayer meeting, and the coordinator asked everyone what God had called them to do. When it came time for me to answer, I said, "I haven't received my calling yet." I was told to continue to pray in the spirit until I hear from God. Can you give me some feedback* *on this issue I'm facing? Whatever God wants me to do, I'm ready, but I want to hear from Him and do what He wants me to do.*

A. First, let me say that God has not called everyone into full-time pulpit ministry—the five-fold ministry positions listed in Ephesians 4:11: *"And he gave some, apostles; and some, prophets; and some, evangelists; and some, pastors and teachers."* In my prayer time as a young child, I sensed the Lord quickening my spirit that I would be in full-time ministry and that I was to marry a minister. As a teenager, I began preparing for the ministry by volunteering in my church in whatever capacity was needed—whether it was working in the nursery, cleaning the church, or washing dishes at the church social.

Not all believers are called into full-time ministry, but we should be working for the Lord by giving of our time and talent. Romans 12:6–8 says, *"We have different gifts, according to the grace given us. If a man's gift is prophesying, let him use it in proportion to his faith. If it is serving, let him serve; if it is teaching, let him teach; if it is encouraging, let him encourage; if it is contributing to the needs of others, let him give generously; if it is leadership, let him govern diligently; if it is showing mercy, let him do it cheerfully"* (NIV).

If God has not spoken to your heart about a specific ministry, then ask yourself: "What natural talent do I have that I can use for the Lord to help further His Kingdom?" Whatever your talent is—music, art, cooking, cleaning, encouraging, or simply being a good listener—be available to volunteer in those areas of the church you attend.

Q. *My husband and I have been married for 40 years. He has always been a person who wants me or someone else to praise him for everything he does. This isn't normal. What would you suggest is the problem he is having? Even though we have children, he still wants to be the center of attention. He is an only child. Maybe you can enlighten me and others who may be going through the same situation.*

A. There could be several reasons for your husband's actions. As an only child, he most likely grew up being the center of attention and became very used to that. When children grow up in a family with several siblings, they quickly learn to share their parents' attention, whereas an only child is not always exposed to this kind of interaction.

Wanting to be praised continually can also be a sign of low self-esteem. Perhaps your husband doesn't feel he has attained the level of success he desires, and he deals with these feelings by placing emphasis on himself and wanting to be praised. Or perhaps he doesn't feel he measures up to your expectations of him as a husband and father.

A basic need of men is admiration. Praise and admiration have a powerful effect on us all. Unfortunately, husbands and wives tend to voice criticism rather than praise. In teaching on marriage, I tell my hearers that we often take our spouse for granted. We need to praise each other daily for what some might consider minor or insignificant things.

I encourage you to communicate your concerns to your spouse. Let him know how much you love him and that you are proud of him. I believe that as you reassure him of your love and appreciation, his need to constantly be praised will diminish.

Prayer:

Father, thank You that I can come to You with every challenge or difficulty and receive Your priceless wisdom and help to change the situation. Please continue to show me how to get the most out of life, in the Name of Jesus.

Thoughts for the Week:

⟋⟋

The Ten Percent Rule

"Bring ye all the tithes into the storehouse, that there may be meat in mine house, and prove me now herewith, saith the Lord of hosts, if I will not open you the windows of heaven, and pour you out a blessing, that there shall not be room enough to receive it."

Malachi 3:10

When I think of the Father's love and mercy for us, and all that His Word tells us He will do for His children, I become overwhelmed by His goodness. I am so grateful for the promises that God has given to us in His Word. Yet those promises that He set down in His Word are much like the promises and privileges that we set down in our homes with our children—there are both rewards and consequences.

A family is a partnership—a give-and-take situation. When we were raising our children, my husband and I established rules and guidelines for them, saying, "When you obey the rules, here are the rewards. If you disobey the rules, here are the consequences." God has set down guidelines for us in His Word. As long as we follow the guidelines, He is obligated to perform His Word. But if we do not obey, God is not obligated to hold up His end of the bargain. One guideline in particular—the giving of tithes and offerings—has often been ignored, so I want to talk about it here.

I'm sure you are familiar with Malachi 3:8–10 that says, *"'Will a man rob God? Yet you rob me . . . in tithes and offerings. . . . Bring the whole tithe into the storehouse, that there may be food in my house. Test me in this,' says the Lord Almighty, 'and see if I will not throw open the floodgates of heaven and pour out so much blessing that you will not have room enough for it'"* (NIV).

Certainly we all want the floodgates of Heaven to be open to us, but surveys have shown that only about 9 percent of born-again Christians actually pay tithes regularly. My parents taught me the importance of tithing and giving offerings when I was a young child. Whenever I received money from my allowance or any other source, my parents reminded me that the first 10 percent belonged to God. I learned the 10 percent rule long before I learned the math principle of percentages in school. The principle of tithing and giving offerings has always been a settled issue with me.

The enemy knows the blessings you will receive when you give to God. He'll try to keep you from receiving those blessings by telling you lies such as, "If you tithe, you won't have enough money this week—you won't be able to pay your bills and you won't be able to eat." I am a living testimony of someone who has tithed and given offerings all of my life, and I have never once been unable to pay a bill, nor have I gone hungry. I may not have always had an abundant supply —but my needs have always been met.

Something I have made a practice of is to always write my tithe check before I figure my budget. I hope you do that too. The reason is that our tithe is our seed. That is really the problem with many people —they are eating their seed.

Look at it this way. A farmer can have a large amount of land. That land may be fertile and able to produce a large crop. It may have an abundance of rain falling on it. The farmer could say, "Thank You, Lord, that I have a lot of land and my land is fertile. Thank You that I have an abundance of rain." Yet if that farmer doesn't plant any seed, he won't reap a harvest.

That's exactly what many Christians are doing. They confess, "Thank You, Father, that I have more than enough and all of my needs are met. Thank You that I am rich and not poor—that my cup is running over." But their confessions are empty because they're not planting their seed by giving their tithes and offerings unto the Lord.

One thing to remember about paying your tithes: the harvest from your sowing won't always come in overnight. It takes time for a farmer to reap a harvest after planting the seed, and the same may apply in your life. But God is faithful; He doesn't break His promises. And He says in Genesis 8:22, *"While the earth remaineth,* [there will be] *seedtime and harvest."* So I encourage you to keep on sowing; if you will, your harvest will come.

Prayer:

Father God, I want to follow Your guidelines and give my tithes and offerings to help further Your kingdom. But no matter how hard I try, I could never outgive You. Thank You that I am reaping an abundant harvest of blessings that only You can give, in the Name of Jesus.

Thoughts for the Week:

_____

_____

_____

_____

Being a Mary in a Martha World

"Those who trust in the Lord will find new strength."

Isaiah 40:31 NLT

Many years ago I became so distracted by the mechanics of getting natural things done that I failed to realize the Lord was there to help me; all I had to do was spend time with Him. My reputation became such that people said, "If you want something done, give it to Lynette. She'll see that it gets done, and that it gets done right." And it's true, because I have always been a perfectionist. I don't delegate very often because I am picky about how things are accomplished. I would rather do them myself than have to undo someone else's imperfections or mistakes. Being a perfectionist, though, can get you into the Martha syndrome in a hurry.

One day Jesus came to Martha's village while traveling. She opened her house to Him and made Him feel at home (Luke 10:38).

Her sister, Mary, *"sat at the Lord's feet listening to what he said. But Martha was distracted by all the preparations that had to be made. She came to him and asked, 'Lord, don't you care that my sister has left me to do the work by myself? Tell her to help me!' 'Martha, Martha,' the Lord answered, 'you are worried and upset about many things, but only one thing is needed. Mary has chosen what is better, and it will not be taken away from her'"* (vv. 39–42 NIV).

Martha was busy doing many good things, but Jesus said that Mary had chosen the better thing to do—spend time with Him.

Now, it's not wrong to be a Martha sometimes. Certainly, work must be accomplished. However, in the midst of the work to be done, we must recognize the importance and value of the example Mary represents. We must learn to bask in the Presence of the Lord God Almighty.

Time and again, I found that when I functioned in my Martha role, I neglected the very tool that made it easy to perform the Martha tasks—communion with my Heavenly Father. And that's a tactic of the enemy. He wants to get you so involved in doing Martha deeds that you don't have time to commune with the Lord. Yet it is vital that you commune with Him on a daily basis.

Communing with the Lord every day doesn't mean you can't perform the Martha tasks as well. You can commune with Him while you are doing them. I spend the time while I'm getting ready in the morning in communion with the Lord. By the time I am ready to leave my home, I have spent 90 minutes talking to God. During that period, I ask Him for wisdom and divine favor, as well as direction for the day. I thank Him for perfect health for my family. I ask Him to give me strength to perform all the necessary tasks of that day. When I do that, I find that I go through my busy days with ease.

So if you are tired, worn out, or feel weak, check up on the amount of time you are spending with the Lord. The prophet Isaiah talked about this, saying, *"Have you never heard? Have you never understood? The Lord is the everlasting God, the Creator of all the earth. He never grows weak or weary. No one can measure the depths of his understanding. He gives power to the weak and strength to the powerless. Even youths will become weak and tired, and young men fall in exhaustion. But those who trust in the Lord will find new strength. They will soar high on wings like eagles. They will run and not grow weary. They will walk and not faint"* (Isa. 40:28–31 NLT).

When summer comes to a close and the activities and busyness of the fall begin (the school year dictates the year's schedule for many of us), it is especially important to understand what this passage is saying to avoid becoming encumbered by the cares of life. God doesn't want you to live with weariness. He wants you to realize that He will give you the strength and ability to perform your tasks each day as you spend time with Him. I know this is true because I've proven it many times in my own life.

People often ask me, "How do you accomplish all that you do?" I simply reply, "I wait upon the Lord." There is no way I could do it all otherwise. So I encourage you to spend time with the Lord every day. As you do, you'll be able to accomplish daily assignments, while allowing the peace of God to reign in your life.

Prayer:

Heavenly Father, forgive me for neglecting to commune with You daily and trying to perform tasks on my own. Help me to bask in Your presence every day so I can receive strength from You to accomplish the work I need to do and abide in Your peace while I'm doing it, in the Name of Jesus.

Thoughts for the Week:

Listen to God's To-Do List

"I will instruct you (says the Lord) and guide you along the best pathway for your life; I will advise you and watch your progress."

Psalm 32:8 TLB

Many years ago, the Lord gave my husband a phrase that he often repeats—"The natural and the supernatural, working together, make an explosive force for God"—and it has been a guiding force in our lives ever since. I realize that we really live in a fast-paced world. In the natural, time can become one of our worst enemies, because it seems that there is never enough time to go around. So I want to focus on both the natural and the supernatural aspects of time management and offer some practical hints that have helped me redeem my time and keep my sanity.

There always seems to be too much to do and not enough hours in the day to accomplish it all. This "time shortage" can cause us to live in a continually stressful environment. So it's important that we keep a natural to-do list. I find that writing down on paper any future tasks I must attend to allows my mind to focus my full attention on whatever I am presently doing. It also helps me to prioritize things. I like to make my list each night for the next day, but you should choose a time that works best for you.

In making a to-do list, you may find you have more on it than you can accomplish in one day. Don't let that frustrate you. Simply move any "not done" items to the next day's list of things to do. When I find that I am consistently getting behind on my list, I ask myself, *Can I delegate any of these items to someone else?*

This kind of delegation would alleviate stress for a lot of people. For instance, many working mothers stay frustrated because they are trying to work, keep the house clean, cook for the family, spend time with their husband and children, and spend time with God. There is absolutely not enough time to do everything and keep your sanity. So what should you do? If you can, assign some of the tasks to someone else!

Every time-management book instructs readers to write a daily to-do list and as you can see, I definitely agree we should do that; I do it on a consistent basis. But we also should ask God to instruct us and guide us in our daily life (Ps. 32:8). It may sound simple, but I daily ask the Lord to guide me in the things I need to accomplish that day, not only for myself but also for Him.

I find that many times God wants to add some things to my to-do list that I might not have included on my own. For example, God may instruct me to speak a word of kindness to the waiter who took my order; to call a friend and encourage her; or to pray for the need of an employee.

If we are not careful, we can get so engrossed in checking off our to-do list that we forget one of the greatest exhortations in the Bible: *"Anxiety in a man's heart weighs it down, but an encouraging word makes it glad"* (Prov. 12:25 AMP). God can bless others through us by guiding us to say an encouraging word at just the right time.

I was so blessed the other day when I received a note from a well-known woman of God whom I have admired for many years. She expressed how much she enjoyed my column and what a blessing I had been to her. This particular day I needed a word of encouragement in the worst way. Her note gave me a lift and helped me tackle the hard tasks and decisions I had to make that day. How vitally important that word was for me on that specific day. And how thankful I was that she had listened to God's to-do list!

It is so important to keep God's to-do list in mind, as well as to have our own list that we commit to paper. If you have not consistently followed a to-do list in the past, I encourage you to try it for a month. I'm sure you'll find that it will not only relieve stress, but when you are able to mark off some or all of the items on your to-do list, it will also give you a sense of accomplishment.

Prayer:

Father God, thank You for instructing me and guiding me in my daily life. Fill me with Your strength and wisdom as I work to accomplish the tasks on my to-do list each day. Help me to listen when You give me something to add to it and to make it my priority to accomplish what You lead me to do, in the Name of Jesus.

Thoughts for the Week:

Your Most Powerful Weapon

"I can do all things through Christ which strengtheneth me."

Philippians 4:13

Every day we speak countless words, but how often do we really pay attention to the words themselves? It is vitally important to realize that we are creating our world by the words we speak. Proverbs 18:21 says, *"Death and life are in the power of the tongue, and they who indulge in it shall eat the fruit of it [for death or life]"* (AMP). I encourage you to take time and reflect upon the kind of words you have been speaking. Are they negative words or positive words? Are they uplifting words or harsh words?

You may wonder why things aren't going well for you. Perhaps you need to put a watch over your lips. You may have created your situation by your own words. That's what Solomon (often called the wisest man who ever lived) said in Proverbs 6:2: *"Thou art snared with the words of thy mouth, thou art taken with the words of thy mouth."*

I have always endeavored to look on the positive side of things, but it's not always easy to do. Often when I am facing a challenging situation, my head wants to say, *This can't be done*, but I don't focus on that thought or feeling. I always allow my heart to speak a confession of faith, saying, *"I can do all things through Christ which strengtheneth me"* (Phil. 4:13).

We need to be careful of the words we speak, not only to ourselves but to our family and other loved ones. Our words can either hurt or heal. They can inspire or destroy. Too often, we speak kindly to strangers, coworkers, or friends but speak harshly to our family. It is so important, for example, that a wife speak uplifting words to her husband as he leaves for work. He will meditate on those words for the rest of the day. The words she speaks to him may determine whether he makes right or wrong decisions that day.

Many years ago, my husband was preparing to leave for an extended missionary trip. I knew he would face challenging conditions where he was going. The children were young at the time, and I knew he would miss his family. So as I was packing his suitcases, I placed encouraging notes among the clothes. Knowing him as I do, I knew he would not unpack all his clothes at the same time, so he would randomly discover the notes throughout his trip. When he returned home, he told me that at the exact time he was homesick, he would discover one of the uplifting notes of encouragement.

We should make it a practice to allow only faith-building, positive words to come forth from our mouth. I encourage you this day to put a watch over your words.

I fondly remember the story I read as a child about the train that fought its way up a steep hill, saying, "I think I can, I think I can." As "the little engine that could" was about to accomplish his mission, he began to exclaim, "I know I can, I know I can." We need to take that same attitude when adverse circumstances come our way.

Your head—your thoughts—may give you a problem. Your head will scream in your ears, "You're going to fail this time!" Your head will say, "You're going under this time!" Sickness and disease may be devouring your body or you may have an unexpected financial crisis and your head will say, "You're not going to make it this time!"

When the devil fiercely attacks your mind, that is when you must allow the written Word of God to flow forth from your mouth. Don't ever face the attacks of the devil with your mouth shut. Your mouth is your most powerful weapon. In the midst of adverse circumstances, boldly declare, "None of these things move me!" That's what the Apostle Paul declared with boldness in

Acts 20:24. Then he said, *"Neither count I my life dear unto myself, so that I might finish my course with joy, and the ministry, which I have received of the Lord Jesus, to testify the gospel of the grace of God."*

Perhaps you have been moved by circumstances that are coming against you. The enemy may be trying his best to deter you from accomplishing the will of God for your life. He may have already caused you to lose your joy. You may have even allowed thoughts such as *life is not worth living anymore* to enter your mind. I admonish you to kick the devil out of your life with the words of your mouth!

Know that *"Greater is he that is in you, than he that is in the world"* (1 John 4:4). With the Greater One living in you, you can't be defeated if you will not quit!

Prayer:

Father God, forgive me for any harmful words I've spoken over myself and to others. Help me to use only words that encourage, heal, build, and cheer up those around me, in the Name of Jesus.

Thoughts for the Week:

_____

_____

_____

Rest, Refresh, Renew

"'Come with me by yourselves to a quiet place and get some rest.'"

Mark 6:31 NIV

When our children were young, it seemed that all of the time my husband and I had outside of our work was consumed with their schedules. To console myself, I would say, "Hang on, Lynette. The time will come when you'll have some time just for yourself." Now that my children are grown and I am the proud grandparent of five grandsons, I still find myself in the position of trying to find time to enjoy a few personal moments in life. Something will always fill your day or week if you will allow it. More often than we care to admit, I think we all find ourselves living a hectic lifestyle and needing time to just enjoy life.

Do you find your schedule so busy that at times you want to throw up your hands and say, "Stop, world, I need a rest"? Jesus understood the importance of taking time to rest. The disciples had been carrying out the mission of Jesus, and at one point they came back to report to Him what they had done and what they had taught. When Jesus saw them, He recognized that they were weary. Mark 6:31 says, *"Then, because so many people were coming and going that they did not even have a chance to eat, [Jesus] said to them, 'Come with me by yourselves to a quiet place and get some rest'"* (NIV).

Often we are not even aware of how tired and weary we are. When that happens, relationships can be affected. That's why if I start to get irritated at people and situations, I know it's an indication that I need to set aside some time to rest. Even marriage problems can begin simply because couples haven't taken the time to get away and relax. You don't have to take a long vacation to do that, either.

My husband and I occasionally go on what we call a "mini-vacation." We simply take a day off and drive through small towns in Oklahoma. We usually do nothing but look at the hills and visit various discount stores in the towns. It's not an elaborate trip—just a time to get away from the stresses of life and simply rest and relax. No matter what you choose to do, you'll be amazed at how just a short time of rest will do wonders for your attitude. It will help you keep things in proper perspective.

Even our decision-making can be affected by a lack of rest. All of us are faced with decisions on a daily basis. Some decisions can be made easily, but other decisions can be of major consequence. I have at times become frustrated because I would seek God's guidance in making the right decision, and it seemed that He wasn't giving me a reply. But when I drew away for a time of rest—a time when I wasn't even concentrating on the situation—God would give me the right solution for the problem.

Many times we don't realize what stress does to our natural body and that we need to take time to rest and relax to be rejuvenated physically. I learned that through an incident that happened in my mid-forties. It seemed that I suddenly didn't have the energy I was used to. I was getting adequate sleep, yet I was still tired. I began to think, *Well, this must be a sign of getting older.* At that time I wasn't even aware of my need to get away from the routine of life's stresses and chores.

My husband and I decided to take a week off and just get away and do nothing. After relaxing for a week with no pressure, not only had I received much direction from the Lord, but I had an abundance of energy. That taught me the importance of setting aside time to rest. I realized my age wasn't the problem. I had worn my body out and needed a time to rest and recuperate.

I want to encourage you to take some time off and rest and refresh your body. It will not happen unless you make the effort to mark out the time and not let anything interrupt your planned retreat. You will find that you will receive a refreshing from the Lord that will help you face the challenges of life.

Prayer:

Lord, forgive me for allowing external demands to make my life hectic and wear me out physically, mentally, and emotionally. When my schedule threatens to sap my energy and leave me stressed, help me to take time off to rest, refresh, and renew myself, in the Name of Jesus.

Thoughts for the Week:

The Bumps Are for Climbing

"Count it all joy when you fall into various trials."

James 1:2 NKJV

When we read the Word of God, it is very easy for us to concentrate on our favorite scriptures. We love to read His promises, and I'm certainly thankful for the promises He has given to His children. Yet there are other verses in the Word that we would just as soon skip over. I know some people who struggle when reading certain chapters in Leviticus in the Old Testament. It is not their favorite book of the Bible. The Book of James is the one that's not a favorite of mine. But there is information in these books that is necessary for our walk with God, such as what's found in James 1:2–4 (AMP):

2 Consider it wholly joyful, my brethren, whenever you are enveloped in or encounter trials of any sort or fall into various temptations.

3 Be assured and understand that the trial and proving of your faith bring out endurance and steadfastness and patience.

4 But let endurance and steadfastness and patience have full play and do a thorough work, so that you may be [people] perfectly and fully developed [with no defects], lacking in nothing.

I'll never forget when I began studying the Book of James many years ago. My husband and I had begun to work for Kenneth Hagin Ministries, and I had been reading many of the faith books written by my father-in-law. I was pumped up in my faith and I felt there wasn't any mountain I could not speak to and remove. Then one day I felt impressed to begin reading James. I read and kept going over chapter 1, verses 2 and 3, on counting it all joy during troubles because they try our faith and build patience in us. I had been reading the Word and had received knowledge of it. Now came the time of testing (or trying) my faith to see if I would be a doer of the Word and not just a hearer (v. 22).

Faith is based on the Word of God, but proof of faith comes from living the life of faith. So our faith will be tried—and not just once and then it's over for life. Our faith will be tested again and again. God never promised us a life without trials, but He has promised in Psalm 91:15, *"He shall call upon me, and I will answer him: I will be with him in trouble; I will deliver him, and honour him."* And again in Isaiah 43:2, *"When thou passest through the waters, I will be with thee; and through the rivers, they shall not overflow thee: when thou walkest through the fire, thou shalt not be burned; neither shall the flame kindle upon thee."* Our life must be based on faith in our Heavenly Father. Everything else around us may fall, but if our faith in Him stands, our life will stand.

The desire of our enemy is to destroy our faith in God. Since the Garden of Eden, Satan has been trying to create in the mind of man the devastating thought that God does not really love us. Satan's plot is to make it appear as if God does not hear or answer prayer. Satan will try to kill your confidence in God, especially when you're going through a trial. He will come to you and say, "See—this faith stuff doesn't work. What happened to your God? You believed, and it didn't work."

The enemy endeavors to get you into the arena of reasoning and doubt. He wants you to start doubting the provision that your Heavenly Father promised you. Actually, the enemy wants to get our eyes off of what he is doing—stealing, killing, and destroying, according to John 10:10. But this verse also says that Jesus came that we *"might have life, and . . . have it more abundantly."* Satan is the destroyer—Christ is the deliverer.

So, what do we do when Satan comes into our lives and tries to steal, kill, and destroy? We stand firm on the promises of

God. Here's a great illustration of this in the story of a little boy who was leading his sister up a rugged mountain path. "Why, this isn't a path at all!" the little girl complained. "It's all rocky and bumpy!" To this her brother replied, "Sure! The bumps are what you climb on."

That is the attitude we must possess. We must take the bumps of life and make them stepping-stones instead of stumbling blocks. With Christ, we can triumph over those bumps. Even in the midst of adverse circumstances we can count it all joy, knowing that our God shall deliver us out of all our trials.

Prayer:

Lord, thank You for Your Word that quiets my heart, fills me with joy, and gives me the faith to keep on trusting You in the face of adversity and troubling times in my life.

Thoughts for the Week:

Choosing a Mate

"In all thy ways acknowledge him, and he shall direct thy paths."

Proverbs 3:6

I often receive letters from people who say they are having a difficult time knowing whom to marry. They desire to have what God has in store for them, they really want to do His will, and they ask me to tell them some things they need to know so they won't miss it. Choosing the person you will share your life with is one of the most important decisions you will ever make.

There are two sides to choosing a mate. The *spiritual side* involves prayer and following the guidance of the Holy Spirit. For example, from the time I was a young child, I knew I was called to the ministry and I told the Lord, "You know the plan for my life. You said in Mark 11:24, *'What things soever ye desire, when ye pray, believe that ye receive them, and ye shall have them.'* God, it is very important to me to marry someone who has the same calling as me. So I trust You to direct my path to the right person."

I also stood on Proverbs 3:5–6 for finding my mate: *"Trust in the Lord with all thine heart; and lean not unto thine own understanding. In all thy ways acknowledge him, and he shall direct thy paths."* We must ask the Lord to direct and lead us in the right direction to find our spouse—and then we need to follow His leading.

Although God does direct our paths, He created us to be free moral agents, and we're free to choose the person to marry. So we do have a part to play. One thing to do is take advantage of opportunities in which you can meet other single Christians. My husband and I developed our relationship through writing letters. He was in the Army then and a mutual friend asked my mother if I would write to him, as he was overseas and receiving little mail. I could have decided not to and our paths might have never crossed.

We often want to tell God how to grant our desires, but He will always do it His way. My human reasoning said, "Lord, I will just keep praying about a mate. I expect You to bring him to me." But something on the inside of me (the prompting of the Holy Spirit) said, "Write to Ken." So I had a part to play. (See James 2:17.) Then God did His part, and Ken and I have been happily married for over 42 years.

There also are *natural things* that you should consider in choosing a mate. When I was single, I compiled a list of attributes that were important to me and that I desired in a mate. The more you both hold in common, the greater the foundation for marriage. Opposites may attract, but in daily living as a married couple, being total opposites can lead to strife and frustration, not harmony—like being limited in recreational times together and not being able to share some of the most important aspects of your lives.

The issue of children should definitely be discussed before marriage. If one of you desires a large family and the other doesn't, that can cause major problems. Another important issue to consider is whether you share the same goals. A couple must move in the same direction toward the same goals in order to be successful in life and marriage.

Unfortunately, many of these issues are not talked about until after the wedding takes place. It's important to make sure you communicate honestly before marriage.

When you do find that special someone, I advise you not to rush into marriage. Get acquainted with that person and see how he or she reacts in different situations and under different stresses in life. While you are still dating, pray that anything hidden concerning your future mate's personality will be revealed. Sometimes a person can be deceptive, and who you think you are marrying is not the true person at all.

Most importantly, marry someone who has accepted Jesus as Lord and Savior. The Bible tells us not to be unequally yoked (2 Cor. 6:14). It is very difficult to become one with a spouse without the common bond of Jesus at the center of the relationship.

I encourage you today to follow these guidelines. God has also set down guidelines in His Word, and as long as we follow them, He will do what He has promised. So *pray* continually (1 Thess. 5:17) during the entire dating process (and make prayer the mainstay of your marriage). *Trust* in the Lord, because as you do, He will direct your paths (Prov. 3:5–6). *Listen* to His voice in your heart and in His Word (John 10:3–5), and He will lead you to the right person with whom to share your life in marriage.

Prayer:

Thank You, Father, for the person You are leading me to so that I can find the right mate. Help me to do all that I need to do, spiritually and naturally, and to trust You to do the rest, in the Name of Jesus.

Thoughts for the Week:

◿

Sorting Out Priorities

"Seek the Kingdom of God above all else, and live righteously,
and he will give you everything you need."

Matthew 6:33 NLT

We live in a busy and complicated world, where most of
us are constantly trying to figure out our priorities. We always
seem to have too much to do and not enough time to do it all.
When I was growing up, my parents were pastors of a church
and my entire life revolved around our church and its activities.
In those days, it seemed there was no life outside of church.
Eventually, because some parents were neglecting their children, parents began to realize that God expected them to care
for their family as well as for the church.

Unfortunately, people could not seem to find a balance
between the two. So instead of neglecting their family, some
people began to concentrate so much on their family (such as

getting their children involved in all types of athletics as well as other extracurricular activities) that the church became neglected and less important than everything else. This was not God's intention either.

Whether we are the parents of young children or a houseful of teens, when it comes to balancing family and church, there seems to be a constant struggle between the two. Both are top priorities, so we must ask ourselves: is reducing our commitments at church for the sake of our families being selfish?

Parents need to sort out their priorities like never before. To be honest, the example some of today's parents are setting for their children is quite disturbing to my husband and me, particularly when they allow everything else to take priority over the functions of the church. We understand how incredibly difficult parenting can be, but by setting this example, parents are teaching their children that everything else has priority over God. Then when their children are grown, these same parents ask us, "Why is my child not serving the Lord?" It may be that they did not make serving the Lord the priority of their life when their children were growing up.

There's no task more important in life than raising children. The years parents have to raise them pass quickly, so it's vital that we make every day count. One scripture that I was taught very early in life was Matthew 6:33, which says, *"But seek ye first the kingdom of God, and his righteousness; and all these things shall be added unto you."* This is the verse I always reference when I need to sort out my priorities.

As a parent, I tried to teach my children that God's Kingdom comes before anything else. My husband and I also endeavored to live a balanced life with our children. We set aside time for church, as well as time for school and family activities. The children were involved in athletic activities, but not to the extent that athletics consumed our entire life. (If parents allow sporting events to consume their children's lives and never build a relationship with them outside the realm of sports, those parents won't have a relationship with their adult children when the years of athletics are over.)

I believe it is easy for people to get in a ditch on either side of the issue—either neglecting family or neglecting the church. In order to find proper balance between the two, I encourage you to look to the Lord, and He will give you wisdom to establish your priorities. (See Eph. 1:17; James 1:5.) He will show you where you can redeem the time and therefore be able to honor your commitments at church and take care of your family as well.

Prayer:

Father God, I want to be a faithful parent and raise my children right to keep eternal priorities first. Give me Your strength for that task and wisdom to know how to balance my family and church. I am letting go of my agenda and timetable for my children's lives. Show me how to teach them that You and Your Kingdom come before anything else, in the Name of Jesus.

Thoughts for the Week:

〜

Our Refuge and Fortress

"[God] is my refuge and my fortress: my God; in him will I trust."

Psalm 91:2

With times as perilous as they are, it is important that we all claim the promises of God for protection over our lives. All of us refer to certain scriptures more frequently than others, and one scripture passage that I have always claimed in relation to protection is Psalm 91. Every day I speak it over my entire family. Of course, when we claim this passage of scripture, it is important that we abide by the guidelines. So I want to look at them with you to be sure you understand how they relate to you personally.

First of all, Psalm 91:1–2 says, *"He that dwelleth in the secret place of the most High shall abide under the shadow of the Almighty. I will say of the Lord, He is my refuge and my fortress: my God; in him will I trust."* I like how the *New International Version* puts verse 1: *"He who dwells in the shelter of the Most High will rest in the shadow of the Almighty."* To dwell in the shelter of the Most High means to live in constant communion with God and place Him first in our lives. Doing those two things must become our number one priority if we want the benefits of Psalm 91.

So often Christians neglect their relationship with God; they put it off until a tragedy happens. Then they run back to the shelter of God. We should not live that way. He didn't say to visit Him once in a while; He said to dwell *"in the shelter of the Most High"* (v. 1 NIV). *To dwell* refers to continually inhabiting. In other words, we've got to continually inhabit that secret place in God. It can't be a temporary dwelling; it must be our permanent dwelling place. When we have that kind of relationship with our Heavenly Father, we can boldly claim that He is our refuge and fortress. In times of trouble, we can run to Him confidently, knowing that He will take care of us.

Next, verses 3 and 4 say, *"Surely he shall deliver thee from the snare of the fowler, and from the noisome pestilence. He shall cover thee with his feathers, and under his wings shalt thou trust: his truth shall be thy shield and buckler."* I read those verses for years and heard ministers describe the way a mother hen protects her chicks. But I was not raised on a farm, so it was unfamiliar to me until I saw it happen for myself.

Several years ago, some geese were eating the baby ducks that inhabit our park on the RHEMA campus. So our maintenance staff placed a mother duck and her babies in a pen until the ducklings were old enough to protect themselves. One day I went to check on the baby ducks. I wanted a closer look at them as they played, so I approached the pen. As I came closer, the mother duck sensed what she thought was danger and began frantically gathering the ducklings under her wings. I was amazed at how quickly she covered them until they were out of sight. It was as if she was alone in the pen.

Seeing that verse from Psalm 91 visibly illustrated made an indelible impression upon me. Now I can imagine that happening to me: whatever comes my way, my Heavenly Father so covers me with His protecting arms that the enemy can't find me. This passage assures me that my God will deliver me from any harmful situation or circumstance that may come my way.

I like how the *New Living Translation* puts verses 10 and 11: *"No evil will conquer you; no plague will come near your home. For he will order his angels to protect you wherever you go."* And verse 12 says, *"They will hold you up with their hands so you won't even hurt your foot on a stone."* I quote these verses often, especially when symptoms try to fasten themselves on any member of my family. At those times I quickly tell the devil, "You cannot put that symptom on us, because I have already claimed that no plague can come to our family."

The crowning promises in this psalm are in verses 15 and 16: *"'When they call on me, I will answer; I will be with them in trouble. I will rescue and honor them. I will reward them with a long life and give them my salvation'"* (NLT). I encourage you to take the promises of these scriptures, confess them each day, believe what God has promised, and watch them become a reality in your life.

Prayer:

Heavenly Father, thank You for Your promises of protection for our lives. I confess Psalm 91 over myself and my loved ones and I am resting in Your care, knowing that whatever comes our way, You will cover us with Your protecting arms and deliver us, in the Name of Jesus.

Thoughts for the Week:

A Designer Original

"I have set before you life and death, blessing and cursing; therefore choose life, that both you and your descendents may live."

Deuteronomy 30:19 NKJV

I remember facing a hard time in my life when I had to make a difficult decision. My husband had been working for his father for about two years. Financially speaking, it had been a difficult time for us. Accepting the job had meant a drastic cut in salary, and it had been a constant challenge to pay our monthly bills.

One day while pondering our financial difficulties, I decided that I could do something about it. I had been a hairdresser in previous years, and the Lord had blessed my business during that time. So I thought, *I know what I'll do. I'll go back to work as a hairdresser to help get us out of this financial strain.*

As I sat down at my desk to write a check to transfer my license from Texas to Oklahoma, it suddenly seemed as if I heard an audible voice speak these words to me: "If this is the way that you want Me to provide for you for the rest of your life, so shall it be. The choice is yours."

Needless to say, I started shaking in my boots. Although I had really enjoyed the hairdressing profession, I knew that I didn't want to dress hair for the rest of my life to provide for my financial needs. I suddenly realized that I was about to make a choice—a wrong choice—that would affect me for the rest of my life. I quickly put my pen down and never wrote out that check. Was the financial situation resolved immediately? No, it was not; but through believing God and obeying His plan for our life, a financial breakthrough did eventually manifest.

Each one of us faces choices every day. Sometimes we don't realize the importance of making the right choices. A single choice can make a big difference in our life. Unfortunately, we often make choices on the spur of the moment, according to our emotions, without realizing the effect those choices will have on our future.

My dad made that point clear to me as a child. He would say, "Be careful of the choices you make. Realize that those choices will affect your future. Make sure you are willing to live with the consequences for the rest of your life." Those words of wisdom had a powerful effect on me. Any time I have important decisions to make, his words still ring in my ear, and I always consider what consequences my decisions will have.

Of course, the most important choice anyone can make is the choice of whom we will serve. The choice to accept Jesus as Savior and place Him first in your life is the choice with eternal consequences. It is not only important that we choose to serve the Lord; it is important that we choose to serve Him with our whole heart. Some people serve Him in the good times, but when adversity comes their way, they turn their back on Him.

This is exactly what the enemy wants us to do. But we must be like Job in the Bible. He trusted God regardless of what the enemy brought against him—and so must we. The Lord did not promise to remove all the hard places from life, but He did promise that He would take us to the other side if we put our trust in Him. I saw Him do that for me when we were facing that financial difficulty, and I know He can do it for you!

Do decisions you need to make weigh heavily on your mind? Have you considered how the consequences of your choices may affect you for years to come? I want to encourage you today— don't make choices based on your own natural reasoning. Trust the Lord. Proverbs 3:5–6 says, *"Trust in the Lord with all thine heart; and lean not unto thine own understanding. In all thy ways acknowledge him, and he shall direct thy paths."* Look to the Lord for wisdom. James 1:5 says, *"If any of you lack wisdom, let him ask of God, that giveth to all men liberally, and upbraideth not; and it shall be given him."* Ask the Lord every day for wisdom to make the right choices in life.

If you will look to the Lord for direction, He will never lead you down the wrong path. Don't resist His promptings and leadings, but know that He has a chosen path designed for you. If you'll look to Him and allow Him to direct your choices in life, you will always come out victorious in the end.

Prayer:

Thank You, Father, for Your timeless wisdom that I can follow to help me make right choices in life. Show me the direction You want me to take in every decision I must make, in the Name of Jesus.

Thoughts for the Week:

_____

_____

_____

_____

≈

When Lemons
Become Lemonade

"I have learned how to be content (satisfied to the point where
I am not disturbed or disquieted) in whatever state I am."

Philippians 4:11 AMP

If anything is universal in the day in which we live, I believe
it is discontentment. The old adage "The grass is greener on
the other side of the fence" is well-believed by most people.
Discontentment is very much a part of non-Christians' lives,
for they have not found the One Who can give them peace. But
they aren't the only ones with this grass-is-greener mentality.
I have seen discontentment becoming an increasing problem
among Christians as well.

It seems that we are never pleased. If we are single, we want
to be married. If we are married, we want to be single. If we
don't have children, we want them. If we have children, we

think life would be bliss without them. Jane wishes her husband was like Sally's, and Sally wishes her husband was like Jane's. Fred wishes he could have a new car like Bob's, and Bob wishes he could have a new pick-up truck like Fred's.

The Apostle Paul addressed this in Philippians 4:10 and 11, saying, *"But I rejoiced in the Lord greatly, that now at the last your care of me hath flourished again; wherein ye were also careful, but ye lacked opportunity. Not that I speak in respect of want: for I have learned, in whatsoever state I am, therewith to be content."* Paul was expressing his sentiments to the church at Philippi for the gifts he had received from them. But even though he was thankful for the gifts, he went on to explain, "I am not dependent on this. I know how to live with little or with a bountiful supply. Whichever way it is in life, it's not going to move me from my relationship with God. I am going to be content in whatever situation I find myself."

Some would take Paul's statement to be negative, yet it was far from negative. One of life's greatest victories is to be content in the sense that Paul was content. *Contentment* means freedom—freedom from care, freedom from discomfort. *Contentment* is gratification to the point where one is not disturbed or disquieted—even though every desire is not fully realized.

Actually Paul was telling them (and us), "I choose to be master of my situation, to conquer any circumstances that come my way. I choose to live in peace regardless of my situation." Too many people have this in reverse order. They allow their situation to master them. They allow their circumstances to conquer them. The truth is, you determine your destiny by the decisions you make and the attitude you take. You can choose to look at the positive side of circumstances or the negative side.

I'm sure you've heard that old saying, "When life gives you lemons—make lemonade!" It's important to remember it in this context: When you focus your eyes on the positive instead of on the negative, you get a better perspective of the situation you are encountering. That is something I've taught my own children.

When my children were young, they often came to me with challenging situations they were facing. Sometimes they were distraught over something that was going on in their lives. I always told them, "Let's look at what positive things can come from this negative situation."

Of course, the most important thing you can do in order to live a life of contentment is to be fully committed to God. Matthew 6:33 says, *"But seek ye first the kingdom of God, and his righteousness; and all these things shall be added unto you."* Learn to always place God first in your life. Allow Him to guide your every step.

Your life may not always go down the path that you desire. However, if you will make the determination to seek the things of God, and to be content regardless of the situations you may encounter, you will find that peace and contentment will become a natural part of your life. You can rest assured that God will turn all things around for your good if you'll but trust in Him (Rom. 8:28).

Prayer:

Heavenly Father, I want to be content, regardless of my circumstances. Help me always to seek You first and rest in Your promise to turn everything around for my good, in the Name of Jesus.

Thoughts for the Week:

You Are Amazing!

"I will praise thee; for I am fearfully and wonderfully made."

Psalm 139:14

A teacher once asked her class of 11-year-olds, "What is here in the world today that was not here 15 years ago?" She expected them to tell of some new invention or discovery. One boy quickly raised his hand and replied, "Me!" How right he was! It is important to feel good about yourself. For one thing, in order to complete the work that God has for you, you must believe that you can accomplish His plan. That is a key to walking it out. Yet often people are defeated in life because they have a low self-image, or they don't believe in themselves.

As a child, you may have heard the words, "You'll never amount to anything. You'll be nothing but a failure. You're ugly—fat—dumb." These negative words may still echo in your ears every time you try to succeed at something. It is time to free yourself from that negative influence. You do that by seeing yourself as God sees you. When you start thinking of yourself the way that little boy did, you will suddenly have a different outlook on life. You will realize that you are special to God and that He has a divine purpose for you.

The Living Bible puts Psalm 139:14 this way: *"Thank you for making me so wonderfully complex! It is amazing to think about. Your workmanship is marvelous—and how well I know it."* The psalmist David praised God for His workmanship. We should do the same.

God made you the way you are—and He never created a failure. You have success hidden on the inside of you. It is important that you have confidence in your ability and in God's ability. When you trust in God's ability, the success He created on the inside of you will be manifested in your life.

Philippians 4:13 is the scripture that has helped me believe that I could be a success in life. It says, *"I can do all things through Christ which strengtheneth me."* Many times when I thought I couldn't complete the task God had placed before me, I quoted that verse. The enemy often screamed in my ear, "The job is too big for your ability." I just screamed right back at him, "It might be too big for my ability, but I can do all things through Christ Who strengthens me! It is not beyond God's ability in me!"

Some people use the excuse, "If only I had such and such, I would be a success." None of us can live our life by what we don't have. Start living your life with what you *do* have—and make your life a success. What did the Apostle Peter say to the man at the Gate Beautiful? *"Silver and gold have I none; but such as I have give I thee"* (Acts 3:6). Recognize your abilities, gifts, and strengths—and strive to maximize their use. Take the talents you do have and use them in your natural life, and most definitely dedicate them to the Lord to be used for His service.

Set your goals high. My father-in-law used to say, "I'd rather set my goals high and reach some of them than have no goals at all and reach all of them." If you have not set goals in life yet, perhaps you are afraid of failure. Many people feel the same way. Remember, failures are never final. You haven't failed until you fail to get up. Rise every time you fall. In fact, it's biblical. Micah 7:8 says, *"When I fall, I shall arise."* No person likes to fail, but trying and failing is better than not trying at all. Recognize failures as opportunities. You do not win in life because you never make mistakes; you learn through mistakes how to win. Start living this way and see the difference it makes in your life.

So be proud of who you are. Don't try to be a clone of someone else. You are an individual. There is something you alone can do—some special reason for you to be alive. You are unique, unlike any other person who is alive now or who will ever live in the future. Thank the Lord for His creation and begin to walk out His plan for you today!

Prayer:

Heavenly Father, thank You for who You created me to be and for the wonderful plan You have for my life. I am looking forward to walking it out with You.

Thoughts for the Week:

_____

_____

_____

_____

_____

_____

_____

Comforting Power

"God is our refuge and strength, a very present help in trouble."

Psalm 46:1

Over the years I have truly experienced the wonderful, comforting power of the Holy Spirit. I've always relied on the Holy Spirit to be my Helper, Counselor, and Strengthener, but I never had such great opportunity to experience Him as my Comforter as I did with the passing of my father in 2002. Then, in 2003, my father-in-law, Kenneth E. Hagin, went to be with the Lord; in November 2004, my sister's husband died unexpectedly of a heart attack; and in 2007 my mother-in-law passed away. I have certainly had to rely on the Holy Spirit's comforting power during these times.

They were indeed challenging years for our family. Facing those losses in addition to our normal family and ministry responsibilities, we were often stretched to the limit. Yet as I reflect back upon those years, a certain song comes to mind: "Great Is Thy Faithfulness."[1] God was so faithful to us during those times of great loss—and the strength and comfort of the Holy Spirit were always there.

Through my own experiences, I have found that there are some misconceptions about how Christians should handle personal loss. Some say we shouldn't sorrow at the death of our loved ones. Certainly, we should not allow a spirit of grief to overcome us, but the Bible doesn't say that we shouldn't sorrow. It says that we should not sorrow as those who do not have the promise of eternal life with God (1 Thess. 4:13). That verse doesn't mean we aren't allowed to cry at times when we think of our loved one. Tears are the body's safety valve to release built-up emotions and are vital to the healing process. So surely we are allowed to weep when our friends or family members depart.

Another misconception involves talking about the deceased. I used to be uncomfortable mentioning anyone's relative who had passed away. But after personally experiencing the loss of a loved one, I realized that talking about the departed person is important. It's a healing balm. Through the years my husband and I have laughed about funny things concerning our dads, and we've shed tears during times we miss them most.

When someone you know loses a loved one, you may find yourself as I once did—at a loss for words to express condolences to them. I often said such things as, "He's in a far better place" or

"She's no longer in pain." When my father died, I realized how comfortless those words can be. We have good intentions, and those statements are true for loved ones who accepted Jesus as Savior. Yet those words didn't comfort me when I lost my dad and knew I couldn't talk to him again on this earth. I believe they don't comfort others, either.

Until people personally experience the death of a loved one, it is difficult for them to understand the vacancy it leaves in one's life or the depth of pain a bereaved person feels. I liken the physical separation experienced by losing someone through death to that of a mother and child when the umbilical cord is cut at birth. When a loved one dies, the "earthly umbilical cord" is cut—I am separated from that person and no longer able to enjoy his or her company on earth. And it takes time to heal such a void.

If you are dealing with the loss of a loved one, I encourage you to draw upon the comforting power of the Holy Spirit. I have experienced it often, especially during those times. On those occasions I have also stood on the truth of Psalm 46:1: *"God is our refuge and strength, a very present help in trouble."* It is a comfort to know that He is always there for us. All we have to do is ask for His help.

It is good to remember this too: When the unexpected death of a loved one occurs, people are often tempted to play the "what if" and "why" game. Those kinds of questions only bring turmoil, not peace. As heart-wrenching as the situation may be, it cannot be changed. So it is important to direct your thoughts positively toward God and His Word in order to find peace in the midst of the storm. The Apostle Paul told us what we should think upon—things that are good, pure, perfect, and lovely—*"and the God of peace shall be with you"* (Phil. 4:8–9). He chose to look to God and dwell on the good instead of on any crises that came his way—and God always saw him through.

I encourage you to dwell on good thoughts no matter what, and move out of the arena of questioning God. Begin to focus on His faithfulness and choose to trust in Him. He can give you peace in the midst of every storm and see you safely to the other side.

Prayer:

Lord Jesus, thank You for sending the Holy Spirit as our Comforter. It is comforting to know that He is always there for me, especially during painful times of loss. Help me to demonstrate Your love and compassion to others around me who are suffering loss too.

Thoughts for the Week:

WEEK 42

Use Your Influence

"Train up a child in the way he should go: and when he is old, he will not depart from it."

Proverbs 22:6

Many Christians have become so wrapped up in their own work and life that they have neglected their highest calling—the spiritual development of their children. Parents have the most powerful influence in a child's life. That gives those of us who are parents an awesome responsibility to prepare our children for success in life. I would like to give you a few guidelines on how to do that.

First and most important is to acquaint your children with the Heavenly Father. The verse that my parents instilled in me—*"Seek ye first the kingdom of God, and his righteousness; and all these things shall be added unto you"* (Matt. 6:33)—has been the guiding force of my life. I am so thankful that they continually emphasized that principle to me. The repetition constantly reminded me that God must have first place in my life.

Second, parents need to begin training their children at birth. Did you know that much of the foundation of a child's spiritual and character development is laid during infancy? Experts say that 50 percent of it is formed by the time he or she is three, and 75 percent by age five. Those facts may be startling, but they remind us that we must begin early to guide our children in their spiritual and character development.

Family devotions are an important part of spiritual development. Our family gathered for devotions every morning before school and read the *Faith Food* devotional published by our ministry. After making the daily confessions in it, we would ask each child what they desired to come to pass and would encourage them to make their own personal confessions. It was always exciting to see those confessions become realities for them.

Child specialists agree that every human being has a need to be loved, and meeting that need is basic to proper development. A parent's love is always more important to a child than wealth, education, or any kind of material possession, but a parent's love is most important to a child when that child is the least lovable.

A word of caution about love: you should not condition your love upon your child's good behavior. A child's willingness to please should not determine parental love. The God-kind of love is unconditional. The most important thing is to love your children because they are yours—not because they play the trumpet well or are in the accelerated program at school or they're great at sports.

I can't emphasize enough these next three points. *Don't demand perfection from your child.* That is unreasonable. When children consistently fail to meet their parents' expectations, they lose confidence in themselves and in life. *Don't try to live your unfulfilled dreams through your children.* Some parents do that by demanding that their children do extremely well in an area in which the parents regret not applying themselves. *Don't compare children with their siblings.* A child who grows up in the shadow of a brilliant sister or brother may have a hard time with self-image.

Something else I strongly encourage is that you attend church together as a family. Go to a church that meets the needs of each family member. This is especially important when your children are teenagers. Your church should minister to the needs of the whole family, so keep your children in mind as you select which church to attend. If each family member becomes involved in the church, that will make attending church meaningful and important to every one of you.

Lastly, prepare your children for their roles as adults. Children learn by imitation, so make sure you are giving them the right things to imitate—especially in marriage. Teach them how to make good decisions, and train them in financial affairs. Believe in your children. Speak positive words into their lives. Remind them that with God they can succeed in life. When a crisis comes involving your children, look to the Lord for direction. Trust Him to give you the right words to say and the right actions to take to turn that situation into a victory in your home.

Prayer:

Thank You, Lord, for Your wonderful gift of children. Fill me daily with Your wisdom, strength, love, and guidance; and show me how to nurture and prepare this child You have entrusted to my care for a successful life, in the Name of Jesus.

Thoughts for the Week:

_____

_____

_____

_____

~~

Press In to God

"Delight thyself also in the Lord; and he shall give thee the desires of thine heart."

Psalm 37:4–5

I remember when my husband and I began traveling with my father-in-law back in the early '70s and he was bringing the message of faith to the world. I watched people grab hold of the message and see their lives transformed. They were full of joy as they believed God and He turned things around for them. People were flocking to churches with a hunger to hear more of God's Word. But I'm not seeing Christians exercising their faith as they once did. Nowadays they make a confession of faith, but if they don't get what they are believing for quickly, they give up on that desire.

The main reason for this change is that as the years have gone by, the same people who believed and received from God now fill their lives with other priorities. God and His things have taken a back seat. I believe that it is time to get back to the hunger that we once had for God and His Word—and with the intensity that we have when we really desire something. We make every effort and any sacrifice to bring that desire to pass, whether it is convenient or not, because we are committed to fulfilling that desire.

One of my favorite Bible stories tells of a woman with an issue of blood who had that kind of desire for healing (Mark 5:25–34). This woman's desire was so strong that it overrode all the inconveniences and difficulties she encountered in getting to Jesus. Jewish law stated that she wasn't supposed to be in the crowd in her condition. And she must have been very weak from suffering with the condition for 12 years. Now, if your body is weak, the last place you want to be is in a crowd. Yet she had heard that Jesus was passing by, and she knew that her future depended on her encounter with Him.

She had faith that if she could touch just the hem of His garment, she would be healed. She pushed her way through the crowd, not discouraged at the many people around her who might have been pushing ahead of her, trying to get to Jesus themselves.

That little woman did not give up. She kept pressing in until she finally did what she had come to do—she touched the hem of Jesus' garment. The instant she did, Jesus was aware that virtue, or power, had gone from His body. When He finally found out who had touched Him with her faith, He said, *"Daughter, thy faith hath made thee whole; go in peace, and be whole of thy plague"* (v. 34). She had continued to press in until she received what she desired—healing for her body.

I want to encourage you to get back to pressing in to receive those desires you have had in your heart. You may have begun in faith and gotten discouraged along the way. You may have grown impatient and decided that the fulfillment of those desires was too long in coming. But God's ways are so much higher than our ways, and His timetable is not always our timetable. You may not receive the desires on your list when you want them, but if you won't let your faith waver, He will grant you the desires of your heart.

One scripture passage that I have stood on all of my life is Psalm 37:4–5: *"Delight thyself also in the Lord: and he shall give thee the desires of thine heart. Commit thy way unto the Lord; trust also in him; and he shall bring it to pass."* The three key words in these verses are *delight, commit,* and *trust.* In order to do those things, we must first have a relationship with our Heavenly

Father. He desires that we commune with Him regularly. Communing with Him should be as consistent a part of our daily routine as brushing our teeth.

When you are delighting yourself in the Lord, it becomes very easy to commit your life into His hands. It also becomes natural for you to trust the One in Whom you are delighting. Then you can rest, confident that He will grant the desires of your heart. So press in to God and His things and watch those desires become realities in your life.

Prayer:

Father, I'm sorry for being impatient and discouraged over circumstances I've prayed about. I know that You are faithful to keep Your promises. Help me not to waver in faith, and strengthen me to delight in You, commit every circumstance to You, and trust Your timing in every situation, in the Name of Jesus.

Thoughts for the Week:

_____

_____

_____

_____

↗

Give Thanks Every Day

"It is a good thing to give thanks unto the Lord, and to sing praises unto thy name."

Psalm 92:1

Too often in the midst of daily life, we neglect giving thanks unto our Lord. It seems that instead of thanking Him, we are continually asking of Him. I am sure that our Heavenly Father feels the same way we natural parents do when we become weary of our children asking for things. We wish that they would just thank us for what we've already done for them. Consider the Thanksgiving holiday: many Americans observe Thanksgiving, but somehow the true reason for the holiday has been forgotten.

Originally the holiday was created by our forefathers as a day set aside to give thanks to God for bringing them through a critical year. In today's culture, though, it's just another day off of work for some people; for others it's a chance to get together with friends and family. Many people don't spend the holiday giving thanks to God at all.

I know from personal experience that it's easy for women to be so caught up with preparing the food, the house, and so forth that Thanksgiving becomes a day of dread rather than a day of giving thanks. It seems as though the only moments of gratitude we have for the holiday are at the end of the day when we're just grateful that Thanksgiving is over and we can finally relax!

I want to encourage you as we approach Thanksgiving this year to be careful not to concentrate so much on the "natural part" of the holiday. In other words, instead of wearing yourself out with all the special preparations, spend the day doing as Psalm 92:1 instructs us to do: give thanks and sing praises to the Lord.

King David was constantly praising God throughout the Psalms, and he was called a man after God's own heart. I believe that we should take a lesson from David's habit of praise—and not just when things are going well. Psalm 107:21–22 says, *"Oh that men would praise the Lord for his goodness, and for his wonderful works to the children of men! And let them sacrifice the sacrifices of thanksgiving, and declare his works with rejoicing."* You can see here that sometimes we have to offer "sacrifices" of praise.

We live in a fallen world, which means that there most likely will be times when we won't feel like praising God because of current circumstances affecting our lives. Yet this is the most important time to lift up our voices in praise to Him. Giving God thanks and praise changes our focus from the negative things that may be occurring in our lives to reflecting on all the positive things that God has done for us. I've found that when I'm in difficult situations and I start praising the Lord for the good things in my life, my circumstances start changing for the better.

Philippians 4:8 says, *"Finally, brethren, whatsoever things are true . . . honest . . . just . . . pure . . . lovely . . . of good report . . . think on these things."* When you begin to do what this verse says and praise the Lord instead of complaining—regardless of what you are going through—circumstances in your life can begin to change.

Now, you may not always feel like doing this. Often we would rather question God, asking, "Lord, why are these things happening to me? What have I done to deserve this?" I used to think that way, but here's what I've learned. The devil is roaming around as a lion, seeking whom he may devour (1 Peter 5:8). He wants to get you off track in your thinking and get you to dwell on all the negatives that are occurring in your life. And he wants you to blame God for your difficulties. But let me remind you of something else.

Psalm 91:15 says, *"He shall call upon me, and I will answer him: I will be with him in trouble; I will deliver him, and honour him."* Satan is the oppressor. God is the deliverer! So I encourage you to begin right now, in spite of what you may be going through, to trust in the Lord and thank Him for the good things He has done on your behalf. When you start to praise God— and not just on a once-a-year holiday—you can see each negative situation and circumstance in your life turn around to His glory. That's worth celebrating any day of the year!

Prayer:

Lord, forgive me for neglecting to give You thanks and praise each day. Help me to start fresh and make daily praise and thanksgiving a habit. I want to begin by thanking You for Your love and Your grace and for all the times You've already blessed me, in the Name of Jesus.

Thoughts for the Week:

_____

_____

_____

_____

_____

Speak Pleasant Words

"Pleasant words are as a honeycomb, sweet to the mind and healing to the body."

Proverbs 16:24 AMP

My father used to remind me as a child, "Lynette, be careful of the words you speak. It's hard to take back words once they are spoken." As I got older, I realized that my father had given me very wise counsel, because so many times words can come out of our mouths before we even realize it. That's why it is very important to keep a watch on our words.

Paul the Apostle told us not to let corrupt communication come out of our mouths, but to be sure that we only speak edifying words (Eph. 4:29). King Solomon spoke about words in the Book of Proverbs, saying, *"Pleasant words are as a honeycomb, sweet to the mind and healing to the body"* (Prov. 16:24 AMP). Words can heal or they can wound.

Once as I was seeking the Lord and meditating on His Word, I opened my Bible and the following scripture about words just stood out to me: *"A man has joy by the answer of his mouth, And a word spoken in due season, how good it is!"* (Prov. 15:23 NKJV). I like *The Amplified Bible* version of that. It says, *"A man has joy in making an apt answer, and a word spoken at the right moment—how good it is!"* This reminds me that the words we speak have a powerful influence on others.

Words can devastate or edify; they can build up or tear down. Words can motivate someone to accomplish an impossible task or can cause them to give up in despair. So during Thanksgiving and any other time of the year, I encourage you to look for opportunities to speak pleasant words into the lives of people at the right time. Be sensitive to the needs of others. If you cross the path of a person who needs encouragement, you can ask the Lord to give you just the right word to say.

I've often heard people express their desire for the Lord to use them. You may have that desire too. The truth is, many times the Lord may be trying to use you to minister to someone on a personal basis, but you are oblivious to His urgings. I encourage you to do what I do every day: ask Him to bring people across your path so you can minister words of encouragement and appreciation to them. Then after you pray that prayer, start looking for opportunities to say just the right words to others.

You could begin by speaking an encouraging word to your family members. All too often, we speak uplifting words to everyone but our own family. Many times our words of complaint are spoken so freely to our family. How often do we compliment them for the good things they do. For example, wives should tell their husbands how much they appreciate them. Husbands should do likewise to their wives. Don't let the only words that you speak to your spouse be complaints about what they haven't done. Look for the good qualities in your spouse and compliment those things.

Children offer another wonderful ministry opportunity. Parents should always look for opportunities to speak words of encouragement and appreciation to their children. Instead of always correcting them, a parent should find words to compliment them. If parents begin telling each child that he or she is a success, then those children can rise to the level of the words that have been spoken over them.

Being sensitive to the needs of your coworkers is important too. A simple comment such as "I appreciate you" goes a long way to encourage someone who is having a hard day. I have witnessed the positive effect that little phrase can have on people. An usher who has been with our church from the beginning always smiles and tells everyone he sees at the services, "I appreciate you!" Everyone wants to shake his hand because it encourages them to hear those words. My husband and I always try to tell him how much we appreciate what he does, but he usually beats us to the punch!

Edifying words go a long way. I encourage you to make it a daily practice to find as many opportunities as possible to build people up with words of encouragement, thankfulness, and kindness. You'll find that you will experience joy and satisfaction in your own life because you have ministered to others.

Prayer:

Lord Jesus, it is my heart's desire that You use me to minister to others. I ask You to start bringing people across my path every day who need to be blessed and encouraged so I can speak pleasant words into their lives at just the right time, in the Name of Jesus.

Thoughts for the Week:

_____

_____

_____

_____

WEEK 46

*

Be an
Overcoming Statistic

"In the world you have tribulation . . . but be of good cheer . . .
I have overcome the world."

John 16:33 AMP

One day I was complaining to God about a problem I was encountering, and I said to Him, "Lord, why is it that I just seem to go from one obstacle to another, from one challenge to another? Why is it that I just can't have a time of no adversities?" Have you ever talked that way to the Lord or had those kinds of thoughts?

God spoke ever so loudly to me in my heart, saying, "Haven't you read in My Word the verse that says *'In the world you have tribulation and trials and distress and frustration; but be of good cheer [take courage; be confident, certain, undaunted]! For I have overcome the world. [I have deprived it of power to harm you and have conquered it for you]'?"* (John 16:33 AMP).

The Lord continued, "As long as you are on this earth, you're going to encounter problems." He spoke humorously when He asked, "Which problem would you rather have?" (To us, some problems seem greater than others.) He said, "Quit concentrating on the problem, and keep your eye on the Problem Solver. In Me, you can have perfect peace and confidence, for I have overcome the world for you and deprived it of power to harm you." I'm telling you, that set me free from being constantly burdened down with the everyday cares of life! I realized that the problems I faced were mere distractions to keep me from accomplishing the plan God has for me.

God tells us in His Word that He has a good plan for each of us: *"I know the thoughts and plans that I have for you, says the Lord, thoughts and plans for welfare and peace and not for evil, to give you hope in your final outcome"* (Jer. 29:11 AMP). What disturbs me is that I am seeing many people giving up on that plan or doubting God's plan for their lives. They don't understand the kind of world we live in. We're living in perilous, distressing times in which everything that can be shaken will be shaken.

These are times when the enemy (Satan) is seeking whom he may destroy (1 Peter 5:8), and many are being devoured by him, even Christians. God said in Hosea 4:6, *"My people are destroyed for lack of knowledge,"* so I want you to know that in this natural world, you are going to have trials and tests, *but you don't have to become a defeated statistic.* You can be an overcoming statistic!

Second Corinthians 7:5 says, *"When we arrived in Macedonia, our bodies had no ease or rest, but we were oppressed in every way and afflicted at every turn—fighting and contentions without, dread and fears within [us]"* (AMP). That sounds like our modern-day world. A lack of ease and rest seems to be everywhere. We're stressed out, worn out, and fighting sickness. We have financial concerns, family distress, and concerns about our stability. This outward pressure works on the inside of us until suddenly, we're not only hit from the outside, but inward fears about our life, family, and job begin to dominate us.

No one knew more about adversities and hardships than the Apostle Paul. He faced tremendous obstacles and challenges in life and had every reason to become stressed out and fearful. I think the enemy was continually trying to discourage Paul because he was doing so many great things for God. I believe that God has called every Christian to carry out a tremendous task for Him. So when you step out in faith with big dreams and visions, I guarantee that the enemy will do everything he can to discourage you from accomplishing them. But Paul remained strong in the Lord, and so can we.

If you are going to navigate through the circumstances of life, it is important to take your eyes off the problems and focus on the One Who can solve all of them. When an obstacle comes your way, I encourage you to make this confession: "My Lord has overcome the world for me. My trust is in Him. The battle is not mine, but the Lord's. With God, all things are possible. Many are the afflictions of the righteous, but the Lord delivers me out of them all." As you declare your confessions of faith, you will see the circumstances turn around. You'll walk in peace and confidence, knowing that God will work out all things for your good. And you will fulfill His perfect will in your life.

Prayer:

Father God, I am so thankful that You are my Savior, Healer, and Deliverer from every negative situation. Help me to keep my eyes on You and stay in perfect peace and confidence, knowing that You are working out everything for my good, in the Name of Jesus.

Thoughts for the Week:

From Stressed to Blessed!

"Let them sacrifice thank offerings and tell of his works with songs of joy."

Psalm 107:22 NIV

The United States of America celebrates a holiday that no other nation observes quite as we do—Thanksgiving Day. When I think of Thanksgiving, it is easy for my mind to race ahead and begin to wonder, "How will I ever get everything done for the holiday?" During a usual Thanksgiving, I spend most of the day in the kitchen preparing my family's favorite foods. With all that I have to do, it would be easy for me to get stressed out about the day rather than be thankful for it!

Many of the dishes I cook take time to make. So in order to have the entire menu prepared and ready on time, I have to wake up early in the morning—and that is not my favorite time of day! I also used to stress out because I endeavored to have the meal ready at a certain time. When I didn't meet that deadline, I fretted about it. Several years ago I realized that this stress was causing me to not enjoy the holiday, and I decided to do something about it. An attitude adjustment was all it took to go from stressed to blessed!

Someone once said, "Our minds can shape the way a thing will be because we act according to our expectations." If you begin to think that the holiday will be stressful and a lot of work, that is exactly what it will become. The fact that I must rise so early could start my day out wrong. But instead of getting stressed now, I spend that time alone in the kitchen giving thanks to the Lord for His goodness. As I begin to offer praise to the Heavenly Father, the joy of the Lord becomes my strength—strength to survive the tasks of the day. Instead of dreading all that Thanksgiving Day entails for me, as I praise the Lord, the day becomes one of my favorite times of the year.

Something else I did was to make a simple adjustment of saying, "The meal will be ready when it's ready," which made a huge difference in my attitude. I was no longer uptight about the meal, and getting their favorite foods is all that's important to my family anyway, not the time of day it is served. It amazed me that such a minor adjustment made such a major difference in my attitude.

If you are responsible for preparing the Thanksgiving meal, let me give you a few practical tips that I owe to my mother (a great organized cook!) to help relieve the time crunch. 1) Decide what to serve and write the menu down. 2) Locate all the recipes necessary for the selected items. 3) Do your grocery shopping a week in advance. 4) Set the table on the Monday before Thanksgiving. 5) On Tuesday and Wednesday, prepare any food that can be prepared ahead of time. 6) The night before Thanksgiving, write a to-do list for the next day, listing the tasks in order of completion.

You get the idea. I've found that by doing these things, I am able to carry out my duties and enjoy Thanksgiving Day, stress free.

Getting a meal on the table at a designated time may never bother you, but I am sure that some things in your life are creating attitude problems. I encourage you to take inventory of your attitudes. What is causing you to have attitude problems? Mary Engelbreit[1] has said, "If you don't like something, change it; if you can't change it, change the way you think about it."

I believe that our lives would be a lot more peaceful if we would practice that philosophy. We are able to change many things, just as I changed the time of my meal. Sometimes we just don't take the time to evaluate our attitudes. We fail to understand what is causing us to think as we do. No one enjoys being around someone with a stinky attitude. When I meet someone who is like that, I avoid them whenever possible.

Much of the time our attitudes are affected by constantly thinking on the negative instead of the positive. When Thanksgiving Day approaches, I encourage you to begin to make the holiday a time to reflect on the positive things about your life. Choose to attack every situation with the right attitude, and before the day is over, I guarantee that your right attitude will become a reality for you.

Prayer:

Lord, You have blessed me so much, yet at times I have had a bad attitude, even about the holidays. Help me to adjust my attitude so I can enjoy life instead of being stressed by it, in the Name of Jesus.

Thoughts for the Week:

◞

The Reason for
the Season

"It is more blessed to give than to receive."

Acts 20:35

For most people, the month of December is filled with many festive activities. It is a time for attending parties and other special events and for visiting family and friends. If your calendar looks like mine usually does, you may be wondering if you will have enough time and energy to accomplish all of the month's necessary tasks.

I know firsthand that for wives and mothers, our tasks seem to multiply during the holiday season. We try to get just the perfect gift for everyone on our list. We spend time painstakingly decorating our home, planning festivities for the occasion, and wrapping gifts with perfection. It certainly is very easy to become stressed!

I always spent hours wrapping my packages and would be worn out and stressed out—until the year we were without electricity for two days during the holidays. I had to wrap my packages by flashlight, so I just wrapped them with paper and dispensed with fancy ribbon and bows to save time. My stress diminished so much that I have wrapped that way ever since. I realized that I was stressed and worn out by something that was really unimportant.

In the midst of all the preparation and celebration, I think that we sometimes forget the true meaning of Christmas—celebrating the birth of our Lord and Savior, Jesus Christ. We may not even be aware of it, but we often spend more time trying to find the requested Christmas gifts for our children and grand-children than we spend in teaching them what Christmas is really all about.

My Aunt Oma knew how important that was. I'll always remember that when I was 5 years old, she took time out of her busy schedule during the holiday season to help me memorize the Christmas story from the Word of God. Every Sunday for about a month before Christmas I would go to her home so she could teach it to me.

At times I would have preferred to play instead of go there, but my aunt was very persistent and didn't take no for an answer. It was very important to her that children plant the Word in their hearts. So during the holiday season that year, I continued to go to her house to learn the Christmas story. Then I recited it by memory to the whole congregation at my church. They were truly amazed, and my aunt was so proud of me.

I am very grateful to Aunt Oma for taking time to teach me the Christmas story. It has always kept my focus on the true reason for Christmas. I enjoy giving gifts to my family members just like everyone else does, but I know that Christmas is not about how much we can give to each other. It's about celebrating Jesus' birth and being grateful that God sent His very best gift to redeem mankind who had messed up so badly.

Christmas is such a joyous holiday, but some people don't feel that way. Statistics have proven that Christmastime is when the highest number of suicides are committed. It is a lonely time for those without families who yearn for the fellowship of a loved one. For people who have lost a loved one, it is a time when shared memories and that loss seem to be magnified, as they are more aware that the person is missing from their life. So I want to encourage you that Christmas is the perfect time to get involved in giving to someone in need.

You could even get your children involved. They could take their own money and buy gifts for a less fortunate family. Over the years, we have blessed families during the holiday season, and it is so rewarding to see how grateful they are to be remembered at this time of year. Acts 20:35 says, *"It is more blessed to give than to receive,"* and it is never more true than at Christmastime. How truly rewarding it is to see a smile come to the face of a child who hasn't been experiencing even the basic needs of life.

Take time to focus on the important things. Focus on the joy of giving rather than receiving. Focus on the good memories that you and your family can share together. Focus on giving to those in need. And, most of all, focus on being thankful for the Lord Jesus Christ, Who came into this world to be our Redeemer.

Prayer:

Heavenly Father, thank You so much for giving us Your Son as our Savior and Redeemer. Help me to follow Your example and give to those in need who come across my path—beginning with giving them the gift of Jesus.

Thoughts for the Week:

◌

Childlike Faith

"'Let the little children come to me . . . for the kingdom of
God belongs to such as these. . . . Anyone who will not receive
the kingdom of God like a little child will never enter it.'"

Mark 10:14–15 NIV

I remember the Christmas we gave our son, Craig, a pair of
"jogger skates"—roller skates attached to tennis shoes and made
to be used at a rink. When our daughter, Denise (then 5), saw
them, she immediately wanted some. This was the most expen-
sive gift he had received, and my budget was expended. But I
told her, "When you learn to skate, I'll buy you some."

I thought I was safe because she didn't have a pair of skates
to learn the skill, but surprisingly, she found a cheap set that
Craig had and learned in one week's time. So I honored my word
to her. The point is that never once did she doubt or question
me. She knew that what I said, I would do.

Children are a wonderful gift from the Lord and we need to take a lesson from them. Their hearts are so open to the things of God. Children are not contaminated with all the reasons why something cannot be done. They easily believe the words you speak. In Mark 10:15 Jesus said, *"Anyone who will not receive the kingdom of God like a little child will never enter it'"* (NIV). He was impressing upon us the importance of adults accepting God's promises by simple faith just as children do.

Children live every day on a level of dependence, trust, and faith in someone's words and actions for their needs to be met, but faith comes very naturally for them. God showed us His heart toward children when He said through the Psalmist David, *"Lo, children are an heritage of the Lord: and the fruit of the womb is his reward"* (Ps. 127:3). I believe working with children is one of the highest positions that you can be involved in, and I encourage you to volunteer for that position at the church you attend (if you haven't already). Yet so many churches always seem to have difficulty in getting people to volunteer to work with the children. It's as though some people view that as a lowly position (I hope you are not one of them).

That really grieves me because children have always been so special to me. But the truth is that even the disciples misunderstood the value of children. In Mark 10:13–16 in the *New International Version*, we read, *"People were bringing little children to Jesus to have him touch them, but the disciples rebuked them. When Jesus saw this, he was indignant. He said to them, 'Let the little children come to me, and do not hinder them, for the kingdom of God belongs to such as these. I tell you the truth, anyone who will not receive the kingdom of God like a little child will never enter it.' And he took the children in his arms, put his hands on them and blessed them."* This is another time when we see the heart of God toward these precious little ones.

It is so easy for children to believe and trust because they do not question or try to figure out everything. Isn't that what Jesus told us to do in Mark 11:23–24? He said, *"'If anyone . . . does not doubt in his heart but believes that what he says will happen, it will be done for him. Therefore . . . whatever you ask for in prayer, believe that you have received it, and it will be yours'"* (NIV).

My daughter, Denise, acted like she had received the skates *before* she had them. So it is with the things of God—once you ask in faith, believe that you have received them. The manifestation may not materialize immediately. But continue to believe as a little child does, hold fast to your confession of faith, never doubt God's promises, and it will come to pass.

Prayer:

Lord, help me to appreciate the value of the children You have placed in my life, and to learn from them the childlike faith You approved of, in the Name of Jesus.

Thoughts for the Week:

Practice Peace and Good Will

"Live peacefully with each other."

1 Thessalonians 5:13 NLT

When our schedules are hectic and we are overworked and sleep deprived, it is very easy for us to become cranky and critical of those around us. I've already mentioned the subject of to-do lists, but I know that during busy times and especially the holidays, the list seems so much longer! When I am overloaded with a long to-do list and with time limitations, it is easy for my tolerance level to become very low.

My husband can ask a simple question and my curt response will cause him to ask, "What's wrong with you?" Suddenly I realize that my overload is causing me to respond unfairly to him. I quickly apologize and communicate that it is a busy time and ask him to be patient with me.

My children are grown now, but I still chuckle when I remember hearing my husband say to them, "Don't bother Mom at this time of the year because she is under a lot of pressure." They would tiptoe around the house and try not to ask for any special requests or favors. Often instead of enjoying celebrations and holidays we are wishing that they would soon pass. These special occasions should be a time to enjoy the family. Sadly, some families get together at Christmas or on New Year's Day and simply tolerate the once-a-year tradition to please their parents. Nothing is more disheartening to parents than having adult siblings always fighting among themselves.

The Apostle Paul wrote in First Thessalonians 5:13, *"And live peacefully with each other"* (NLT). Of course we should live in peace with everyone. But it is extremely important that we make peace with our family members. I have heard stories of families who have not spoken to each other in years. That is hard for me to even fathom. Whatever someone may have done to you or said about you, I encourage you to reconcile that relationship. Verse 15 says, *"See that no one pays back evil for evil, but always try to do good to each other and to all people"* (NLT).

I love it when my two children and their families are together with my husband and me during the holiday. I love to fix their favorite foods and watch them "pig out" for the day. Both of my children love my chocolate pie and are so concerned that I may run out that I usually make several. It takes a lot of time since I make the crust and pie filling "from scratch," as my mother would say. But it gives me much pleasure to watch my kids and grandkids devour those pies! It's so gratifying to see my children enjoying each other's company and to watch my grandchildren playing together.

Nothing warms a mother's heart more than having her family members at peace with one another. Maybe you have been estranged from your family for many years. I encourage you to make a decision to reconcile with your family. Mark 11:25–26 says, *"When ye stand praying, forgive, if ye have aught against any: that your Father also which is in heaven may forgive you your trespasses. But if ye do not forgive, neither will your Father which is in heaven forgive your trespasses."*

It is important to forgive those who may have wronged you. If you do not forgive, you are only hurting yourself. Take the first step in the process of reconciliation. Do as Paul admonished in Philippians 3:13: *"Forgetting those things which are behind, and reaching forth unto those things which are before."* Forget those past hurts, forget those past failures, forget the harsh words that have been spoken, and start the slate anew. Say the words, "I'm sorry." It seems that those are the two hardest words for us to vocalize. We never want to be the first one to apologize. You will find, however, that the quicker you accept your part of the blame for the broken relationship, the easier it will be for the other person to reconcile.

Life is too short and family relationships are too important to allow offense to rob you of fellowship with your family members. Make your next special occasion the most memorable one of your life by practicing peace and good will toward all.

Prayer:

Father, forgive me for being cranky and critical to my loved ones. I want to change. Help me to say I'm sorry, even if I don't feel like it, and to make peace with them so we can enjoy each other's company whenever we are together, in the Name of Jesus.

Thoughts for the Week:

⟋

The Light of the World

"If you, then, though you are evil, know how to give good gifts
to your children, how much more will your Father in heaven
give good gifts to those who ask him!"

Matthew 7:11 NIV

One of my favorite events is the Christmas Eve candlelight
service at our church in Broken Arrow, Oklahoma, RHEMA
Bible Church. I love it when the auditorium lights are dimmed
and the only light that remains comes from our glowing
candles. It is such a vivid reminder to me of why Jesus came
into the world.

You see, when mankind messed up, God found a way to
redeem us through the giving of His only Son, the Lord Jesus
Christ. How could we ever doubt God's love for us? It's hard for
us to imagine loving someone so much that we would sacrifice
our only son to save that person's life. But that's exactly what

God did. In all the busyness of the holiday season, it's important to remember that the birth of our Savior and Redeemer is the reason we celebrate Christmas. God gave us His Son to restore our relationship with Him.

As a loving grandparent, I search endlessly to find each of the toys on each of my grandchildren's Christmas wish lists. They are confident that they will find the gifts they have requested under my Christmas tree on Christmas Eve. The thought never even enters their mind that they will not receive their requested gifts. The point is that if we as natural parents and grandparents have such a desire to give to our children, how much more does our Heavenly Father delight in giving to His children! Jesus reassured us of God's love for us when He said, *"If you, then, though you are evil, know how to give good gifts to your children, how much more will your Father in heaven give good gifts to those who ask him!"* (Matt. 7:11 NIV). Not only will God give gifts to us when we ask, He gave us His best Gift—the Lord Jesus Christ—even *before* we asked!

The Christmas Eve candlelight service I mentioned earlier reminds me of this because Jesus came to this world as a gift from God to be the Light of the World for us. That was His mission—and it should be ours too.

I am concerned, especially during the holidays, to see so many Christians focused solely on receiving God's blessings and failing to remember the mission God left for us on this earth. We find the mission that Jesus gave us in Matthew 5:14–16, where He said, *"Ye are the light of the world. A city that is set on an hill cannot be hid. Neither do men light a candle, and put it under a bushel, but on a candlestick; and it giveth light unto all that are in the house. Let your light so shine before men, that they may see your good works, and glorify your Father which is in heaven."*

I feel such a stirring in my spirit about the importance of Christians focusing on witnessing to our world. The world is full of hurting people, and we have the only answer for them: Jesus. It is up to us to present a Savior to these hurting people. God cannot do anything on this earth except through us, His children. I challenge you to accept the mission that our Heavenly Father has given us, and to make it not only the main focus of your Christmas activities but a priority of your everyday life.

I remember a recent Christmas when I was able to witness to someone who unexpectedly crossed my path. But I could have missed the opportunity had I not been willing to take time in the midst of a quick lunch and a busy schedule to become a listening ear. I encourage you to begin to pray for opportunities to be a witness and to become sensitive when the Lord brings an opportunity your way. We can miss these opportunities by being too busy to pick up on His signals and promptings, especially during the holidays.

Remember, you are the light of your world. Let your light burn so brightly that you become an instrument for presenting Christ to those around you. Is there a better Gift than that to give any time of year?

Prayer:

Thank You, Jesus, for bringing me out of darkness and into Your Light. I'm sorry for getting so caught up in the busyness of life and losing focus on why You came to this earth. From now on, I want You to bring opportunities my way to be a witness and an instrument for presenting You to hurting people in my world.

Thoughts for the Week:

A Clean Slate

"Dear brothers and sisters, I have not achieved it, but I focus on this one thing: Forgetting the past and looking forward to what lies ahead."

Philippians 3:13 NLT

I remember as a high school student how bored I was whenever we studied history or geography. At the time I thought, *I'm not ever going to use this information, so why should I remember it?* My solution was to memorize the material in order to pass the tests, and afterward quickly erase the information from my memory. If I had known then that one day I would travel all over the world and how much that information would have benefited me, I would have been serious about learning and absorbing all of it for future reference. Looking back, once I began traveling in ministry, I regretted the choice I had made regarding history and geography.

It seems impossible that another year is just about over. You may be thinking about the last 12 months (or even before that) with regret because of some choices and decisions you have made. We all have made choices or decisions in life that we could look back upon and wish we had made differently. But the Apostle Paul let us know in Philippians chapter 3 that we have a choice in the matter of how to handle them.

I am sure that Paul had some regrets in his life. Before he came to the Lord he was notorious for imprisoning and often killing Christians. Yet once he was born again, he chose to lock the door on yesterday's mistakes and throw away the key.

That is how Paul was able to write these encouraging words to us in Philippians chapter 3, to forget what's behind and reach forth to what's ahead. What are we supposed to forget? I believe we should forget those things that would hinder us from going forward. I like the way the *New Living Translation* puts this because verse 14 refers to running a race and winning: *"I press on to reach the end of the race and receive the heavenly prize."*

It would be silly to think you could win a race running backward. And Paul would not have gone forward if he had continually looked back and dwelt upon his past mistakes. Can you imagine the guilt He would have felt over persecuting the Church earlier in his life? He could have allowed the flashback of those events to haunt him continually. But choosing to forget "those things which are behind" enabled him to go on and write over two-thirds of the New Testament and accomplish many other things for the Lord.

Are you stuck in the past? Then you've made it impossible to accomplish what God has for you now, because you are dwelling on past mistakes and wrong decisions you have made. You are not alone, though. Many people don't realize that they can't change the past—it's sealed in history. But here's the good news: beginning today, you have a clean slate before you. There's just one other thing you must do before you can move forward.

If you haven't already done so, I encourage you to ask God for forgiveness for your past mistakes. First John 1:9 promises, *"If we confess our sins, he is faithful and just to forgive us our sins, and to cleanse us from all unrighteousness."* God is not only *able,* He is *willing* to forgive all your sins. And when He forgives, He forgets—*never to remember them again.* God further promises us in Isaiah 43:25, *"I—yes, I alone—will blot out your sins for my own sake and will never think of them again"* (NLT). He is saying here that once you have asked for forgiveness, your Heavenly Father forgets those sins and never remembers them again. (See Ps. 103:12.)

But the enemy will continue to bring those mental pictures to your remembrance. He has photographs of things that no longer exist and he wants to use them to hinder you from going forward with the Lord. His purpose is to keep you from fulfilling your destiny in life by continually reminding you of your past. So I encourage you to stop looking back! My husband often tells that to our congregation this way: "Turn around and wave 'bye-bye' to your past. Don't ever allow those things to enter your thought life again."

I hope you will take that to heart. And never forget this: we all have made foolish decisions and mistakes that we can't change—but we can learn from them. You may feel that you're not all you should be yet; but be determined that, with God's help, you will never again make the same mistakes. You will focus all your energies on what lies ahead and beyond for you. Remember—God is the God of second chances!

Prayer:

Father, thank You for giving me a clean slate each day to accomplish all that You have planned for my life. Forgive me for any past sins, mistakes, and wrong decisions. I'm excited to press forward with You and see Your plans for me manifest, in the Name of Jesus!

Thoughts for the Week:

PRAYER FOR SALVATION

If you have never accepted Jesus Christ as your Savior, you can do so right now. Pray the following prayer from your heart.

Dear God,

I come to you in the Name of Jesus. I admit that I am not right with You, and I want to be right with You. I ask You to forgive me of all my sins.

The Bible says if I confess with my mouth that Jesus is Lord, and I believe in my heart that You raised Him from the dead, I will be saved (Romans 10:9). I believe with my heart and I confess with my mouth that Jesus is the Lord and Savior of my life. Thank you for saving me!

Signed _____

Date _____

NOTES

Week 3

[1] Andrae Crouch is a well-known, award-winning Christian recording artist and also the pastor of New Christ Memorial Church in San Fernando, California.

[2] "Through It All," *The Best of Andrae*, Andrae Crouch and the Disciples, compact disc, Compendia, 1993.

Week 41

[1] "Great Is Thy Faithfulness," Thomas O. Chisholm and William M. Runyan (Hope Publishing Company, 1923, 1951).

Week 47

[1] Mary Engelbreit is an artist, author, and magazine publisher.

Why should you consider attending

RHEMA
Bible Training Center?

Here are a few good reasons:

- Training at one of the top Spirit-filled Bible schools anywhere
- Teaching based on steadfast faith in God's Word
- Growth in your spiritual walk coupled with practical training in effective ministry
- Specialization in the area of your choosing: Youth or Children's Ministry, Evangelism, Pastoral Care, Missions, or Supportive Ministry
- Optional intensive third-year programs—School of Worship, School of Pastoral Ministry, School of World Missions, and General Extended Studies
- Worldwide ministry opportunities—while you're in school
- An established network of churches and ministries around the world who depend on RHEMA to supply full-time staff and support ministers

Call today for information or application material.
1-888-28-FAITH (1-888-283-2484)
www.rbtc.org

RHEMA Bible Training Center admits students of any race, color, or ethnic origin.